GARAGE-DOOR
Evangelism

Opening Your Church to the Community

by Dary Northrop

Group

Loveland, Colorado

Garage-Door Evangelism
Opening Your Church to the Community

Visit our Web site: www.grouppublishing.com

CREDITS
Editor: Dave Thornton
Contributing Editor: John Fanella
Creative Development Editor: Paul Woods
Chief Creative Officer: Joani Schultz
Copy Editor: Julie Meiklejohn
Cover Art Director: Jeff A. Storm
Cover Designer: Al Furst, Inc.
Cover Photographer: Cambon Photography
Designer and Art Director: Jean Bruns
Computer Graphic Artist: Stephen Beer
Illustrator: Dave Klug
Production Manager: Peggy Naylor

Unless otherwise noted, Scripture taken from the HOLY BIBLE, NEW INTER-NATIONAL VERSION. Copyright © 1973, 1978, 1984 by International Bible Society. Used by permission of Zondervan Publishing House. All rights reserved.

Library of Congress Cataloging-in-Publication Data
Northrop, Dary.
    Garage door evangelism : opening your church to the community / by Dary
    Northrop.
        p. cm.
    ISBN 0-7644-2155-7 (alk. paper)
        1. Church growth. 2. Evangelistic work. 3. Pastoral theology. I. Title.

    BV652.25 .N67 2001
    269.2--dc21
                                                        00-055149

10 9 8 7 6 5 4 3 2 1   10 09 08 07 06 05 04 03 02 01

Printed in the United States of America.

Acknowledgments

I would like to take this opportunity to thank my God for allowing me to partner with him in opening the garage door wide.

I want to thank my wife, Bonnie. She is my lover and my best friend. She has been an encouragement to me in times of real discouragement and despair. She has found ways to make writing this book a possibility.

I want to thank our three children: Ryan, Erica, and Brooke. They have allowed me to focus and complete this task. My prayer is that they will continue to open the garage for their friends to enter in. Kids...I love you!

I want to thank my mom and four sisters who have allowed me to be a different kind of pastor than perhaps the norm. They have loved me and supported me all of my life.

I also want to thank Timberline Church...the Pastoral Team, the Deacon Team, and the entire Leadership Team...you have opened the garage door wide enough to get a whole lot of people inside the house.

Finally, thanks to my editor Dave Thornton. He said I needed to do this project. He stayed with me and encouraged me through many challenging moments, including the loss of over half of this book when my computer crashed. Thanks, Dave!

Let Love Live!

Contents

Introduction

Garage-Door Evangelism was written with great passion and zeal to challenge Christian leaders to rethink the way we "do church." It was written with the understanding that there are some churches in America who have "opened their garage doors" very wide. But it was also written with the realization that the majority of churches are struggling to be effective change agents in a nation that has changed greatly over the past two decades. Most of all, this book was written to encourage Christian leaders who want to go through some transitions in "church" with real purpose and caution.

Many leaders are not saying "no" to church change, they are asking "How?" They seem to have a tenacious desire to make a difference. But the paradigm has shifted so quickly that it is difficult for them to maintain unity in the church and bring meaningful change at the same time.

This book will help Christian leaders find that balance. Too much change too quickly will cause people to feel left behind and bitter. Bringing about no healthy changes will keep Christian leaders from reaching the unchurched world.

THE BIG, BEAUTIFUL HOUSE

Take a look with me at the big, beautiful house on the perfect street with the perfect driveway. It has landscaping that would make a seasoned poodle jealous and a view straight out of a fairy tale! As we look at the house, let's focus in on the front door, framed in majestic oak, surrounded by rounded arches and beautiful glass. The architect designed it this way, you know—to capture the observer, to cause a desperate need to peek inside just once to see the beauty, the décor, the furniture. After all, it's what's on the inside that counts, right? The outer beauty gets our attention, but we need to go beyond the outside. Our human desire is to touch, to taste, and to experience—ah yes, to experience it all!

We're invited into the house, and of course, it's just as we thought—perfect! The furnishings, the surroundings, the carpets, the walls, the trim—everything is perfect! When our tour is finished, we walk away from the house, shaking our heads in awe. The stark reality and the perplexity of hopelessness fill our hearts—"I'll never have a house like that!" We almost wish we hadn't seen it. We were content before touring the dream house.

This picture of perfection has stimulated many emotions. The thrill of seeing what perfection can be leaves us with a nagging disgust that we will never be able to experience it. We feel the hope that maybe it really is possible, but then we experience the reality that we could never attain it.

Thousands and thousands drive by our houses of worship and see the image that we have portrayed. Then they ask the question— "I wonder what it's like on the inside?" You see, the "unchurched" want to touch, taste, feel, and experience the inside—the inside of this beautiful picture we've created for all the world to examine. But they're unsure. They're aware of our statements and slogans. They've watched us over the months, maybe years, and they're hoping that inside there really is a God who loves them. However, the caverns in their hearts tell them that this too is simply a big, beautiful house that would be impossible to attain. Peace? Purpose? Destiny? All of these concepts are seemingly impossible because they've only seen the outside of the house. They're weary of disappointment, and they're afraid they would not meet the criteria to attain the dream we talk about. They're afraid, unsure, and simply weary of the images we call beautiful.

The problem exists because they see and hear our claims and then they meet us personally. There seems to be a difference between what we profess and who we really are. We're real people; broken, divorced, wounded, angry, and jealous. We're people who also get cancer and die. We're people who live on coffee, are overweight, and take Prozac or even use Rogaine! Sometimes we even file for bankruptcy or commit suicide. How can it be? Do our claims really match our lives?

I've been in the ministry now for twenty-one years. I've reached the point of disgust with many easy-answer Christians who want to give the image of complete utopia in every aspect of their lives. I've watched the unchurched examine our statements against our lives and walk away convinced that it is just another scam! In this book,

I'm proposing a very radical, risky concept—being real and opening the garage door, rather than the image-driven front door, to the unchurched. I invite you to examine your own ministry with me as you ask yourself this question—is our garage door open?

Chapter 1

The Garage Door:

THE BIGGEST DOOR INTO THE HOUSE

The garage door is generally the largest door into the house. It's so big that we often forget that it is, in fact, a door. By design, the garage door provides a large entrance into the house. After we enter this large door, we can go into other parts of the house.

But what would happen if the garage door was the *only* door into our house? Imagine it. A beautiful house with only one way to get in—through the garage. This would create a real dilemma. Imagine bringing people over to your house and explaining that because you didn't put a front door on the house, they'd have to enter through the garage. How would architects deal with this new design challenge?

Think of the impact this would have on our home's décor. We usually like to make the entrance to our home the most impressive part. After all, this is where our guests will be arriving. I don't know about you, but when we have company, my wife makes me close the garage door—she's afraid someone might catch a glimpse of the mess inside.

Open Your Church's Garage Door

Let's apply this simple concept to the church: We typically like to make a good, solid first impression. The entrance is decorated and polished. We want to keep it clean so that first-time guests will have a good image in their minds of the church. But what if we took them into the church through the garage door? I know, I know—our churches don't have garage doors. I'm talking theory here. What if we did away with the polished image altogether? What if we told 'em that we were gonna let 'em in through the garage and "what they see is what they get"? No beautiful décor—no shiny floors, no fancy rugs or pictures—just the plain concrete. Sound kind of risky? Sound kind of fun? This is what I'm proposing we should consider.

Disadvantages of Entering Through the Garage

The biggest disadvantage of bringing people into our house through the garage is that it would expose some of the messes we have created. The garage is the place where we put things that we don't want in our house. It collects things like bikes, lawn mowers, and weed eaters. The truth is, the garage gathers "stuff" we really don't want others to see. If we let people into the garage, they'll catch a glimpse of what we're really like; our interests, our hobbies, our work, the things that bring us joy, and the things that clutter our lives. The garage is like an overgrown glove box.

> **❝ We wear the right clothes, say the right things, and hope to convince others that we are who we would like to become. ❞**

How many people do you know who actually keep gloves in the glove box? If we can get the glove box open to put gloves in it, chances are we'll never get it shut again. It's filled with stuff, stuff that we would throw away if we took the time to look at it.

Why would we let a newcomer come into our house through the garage? They would discover us, they would judge us, and they might even understand who we really are. That's scary for us because of the image we have worked so hard to protect. We wear the right clothes, say the right things, and hope to convince others that we are who we would like to become.

Another disadvantage in bringing people into our house through the garage door is that we would become vulnerable. People would be able to discern for themselves the deep and unique things about us. We would be examined like a bleeding patient is examined by a doctor. We'd be discovered and analyzed based upon the facts people see.

Another disadvantage to consider is a lack of preparedness. The garage typically gets a good cleaning when we are sick of the mess. The inside of the house gets straightened and cleaned more consistently and frequently. We're prepared more often for the front-door visitor than we are for the garage guest. One of the first things that happens when someone walks into our garage is an apology: "I'm so sorry about this mess out here in the garage. I'm getting ready to clean it." Liar. The truth is that you would clean it only if you knew someone was going to look at it! That's just human nature.

Advantages of Entering Through the Garage

One advantage of bringing people into our house through the garage is that they could immediately discover things about us that we may never tell them. They may ask questions like "Do you enjoy gardening?" (my wife's corner, I might add) or "Do you enjoy bicycles, or motorcycles, or woodcrafts, or mowing the yard?" Beyond the questions, they may make observations like "They're really organized" or "This place is filthy." As they look around, they may see a cheap garage sale mower or an expensive riding mower. Do we really want people to form opinions of us before we even have a chance to present ourselves? Never! But think of the church—it might be an advantage to let people come into an atmosphere of garage experiences rather than an atmosphere of etched glass, oak doors, and monogrammed mats!

Let me explain—I'm not really thinking about the style or architecture or appearance of your church. I think we should do a great job cleaning, preparing, decorating, and equipping our church buildings. I'm talking about the atmosphere of your church. Atmosphere is that comfort or discomfort that you feel the moment you experience a new place. I've heard people say that it only takes us a few minutes to analyze our surroundings and determine our comfort or discomfort.

I remember our first visit to Universal Studios. As we approached the park, we saw signs pointing us in the right direction. It brought me great comfort to know that we would be directed methodically to the site. I had no stress about getting there because things were so well-marked and identified. As we entered the parking lot, people were there to assist and direct us. We parked in the King Kong section of the parking garage. When we opened the doors of the car we all noticed a big growl coming through the speakers in the parking garage. We weren't even in the park yet and we had already encountered King Kong. It created an "atmosphere." I realize that we're not promoting a theme park featuring King Kong—the truth is, we're promoting the real King of Kings.

> **" So often we miss opportunities with people because we fail to plant comfort and ease in their hearts right from the beginning. "**

So often we miss opportunities with people because we fail to plant comfort and ease in their hearts right from the beginning.

People are growing more finicky all the time. They're aware of their surroundings and are sensitive to atmosphere. Here in Colorado, we have several entertainment centers focused around a cowboy theme. These chuck-wagon-type ranches serve dinner and provide authentic cowboy music. Visitors to these entertainment centers are not greeted with a King Kong growl but rather by a friendly cowboy. These places create a compelling atmosphere a guest *wants* to experience.

Authentic Atmosphere

People in this post-modern era want to feel and experience an authentic faith. Our culture is keenly aware of "atmosphere." Atmosphere awareness is what happens when you drive down the street in a new city at night and things just don't feel very comfortable. You come to a dead end and have trouble turning around. People walk by and stare. You lock the doors because something just isn't quite right. You have that feeling about things. There may be no obvious danger, but it just doesn't feel comfortable. People of this generation have incredible atmosphere awareness. They come into our churches and get a sense about things very quickly.

We've developed this atmosphere awareness because of the dangers in our culture. We've been forced to pay attention in order to protect ourselves from being victims of violence, lawsuits, Internet theft, and various scams. People in this culture have cultivated "street smarts" like a lioness cub on her first hunt. In our culture today, deception is everywhere. We're not really certain if we're eating what we ordered. We don't know what foods cause cancer or even what gender someone really is without an examination. We live in a culture of deception and trickery.

When people visit a church for the first time in this kind of culture, they come with all kinds of sensitivities. They may decide to leave after they walk from the parking lot to the front door. They notice everything, including people's attire, the temperature, the service times, the nursery, the bathrooms, the music, the carpet, the chairs, and the smells. Wow! It makes us nervous to even think about the atmosphere of our church.

In a culture this sensitive, we must make certain that we are who we say we are. This is why it's so important to be careful about our claims. We need to ask some hard questions about what we promote and who we represent. Christians often make personal claims that set them up for close scrutiny. We must communicate in ways that bring people toward us rather than push them away. This is so important because of the resistance people have to releasing their trust to another...especially to a pastor. The fallen media evangelists have created confusion and criticism. Think about it. We preach a sermon that a first-time guest is asked to listen to without knowing anything about us. Can we expect that person to embrace our message before having sufficient time to establish trust in us?

Key Leadership Traits

I would like to suggest several leadership traits for pastors. These concepts are not slick and polished. They're raw and difficult. The suggested adjustments may take some time. As you read, consider how your style of leadership aligns with these traits.

VULNERABILITY

Vulnerable means: "Not protected against harm or injury. Susceptible to attack; assailable. Easily affected or hurt, as by criticism." These are difficult words for a Christian leader to live by.

We'd much rather be known for our ability to find a phone booth and put on the suit with the big S across our chest. "Super Pastor" seems much nicer than "easily affected or hurt, as by criticism."

In a recent sermon, I opened with the fact that Bonnie (my wife) and I had been "in a fight a few days ago." I specifically used the word "fight" to draw attention to the fact that our marriage is like anyone else's. I made it clear that no one was physically injured and no physical scars were apparent. There was a light chuckle across the room. The chuckle came because every person in the room had felt that kind of tension in their relationships. It was true. Sharing this simple incident helped to bring the first-time guest into a place of trust. I wasn't trying to produce the image of perfection but rather one of honesty and vulnerability.

> **66** To practice vulnerability is to open the garage door for people to look around. **99**

A strange thing happens when we allow ourselves to be vulnerable. We actually create hope in people who view us as more spiritual than we are. We use the position of trust to relate truth in a receivable way. Honesty about weakness is often the very thing that allows us to speak truth into another person's heart. We must understand that the Christian life is a risk. When we face this risk honestly and share with others from a vulnerable position, we open up the hearts and the minds of those who come in to judge and find fault with us. When we admit our faults before others discover them, we succeed in building a bridge of trust to them. To practice vulnerability is to open the garage door for people to look around.

TRANSPARENCY

Transparency does not mean spilling your guts in every sermon or sabotaging meetings by sharing all of your stresses. These actions reveal a manipulative attempt to gain sympathy. Real transparency has to do with authenticity and openness about issues that trouble us. As pastors, we need to express authentic feelings to our people through statements that allow people to see our real hearts.

I attended my first Leadership Network Forum last year. I was in a group with seventeen other pastors who led churches of a similar size. Our moderator asked us to put agenda items on the board that we would like to discuss during the next two days. As I listened to pastors share their hearts and list agenda items, I couldn't believe what I was reading on that board. I turned to the pastor sitting next to me and said, "Everything on that board is my whole life." He looked at me and said, "That's impossible, because that's my whole life." The truth of it is, so many things we deal with are the same. I'm amazed at times at how the enemy has used petty differences among denominations or arguments between charismatics and noncharismatics to keep us from coming together to lead effectively. It doesn't always feel comfortable to let our guard down and let people look into our garage, particularly when we let other pastors take a look.

In that Leadership Network meeting, I listened to pastors begin to share their hearts. I listened and I looked into the garages of their lives—I saw their clutter, I saw the pain, I saw the rejection, I saw the hurt, and I saw all the things I've felt in my own life. I related to many of the things on the workbench and in the cluttered glove box. I realized the truth—that we all are very similar. The garage door must open. People must be allowed to look around in that garage to see what that house is really about. I believe that if we learn to expose ourselves, God won't have to expose us.

My congregation knows that I'm not very patient while driving in traffic or when I'm behind a slow driver. They laugh with me about these instances, as I've shared them with a laugh from the pulpit. A funny thing happens—when I do this, people relate to me. They suddenly see my humanity and they enjoy it. Quite honestly, some enjoy it more than they should.

If I let people in my garage, they see some of the "mess" I've created for myself and they smile in their hearts because they know that they, too, have a garage. I learned a truth long ago that I have said many times:

> 66 When we practice transparency in our lives and ministries, we open the big garage door and allow people to take a peek. 99

"share a success, build a wall; share a failure, build a bridge." When we practice transparency in our lives and ministries, we open the big garage door and allow people to take a peek.

TRUST

When I give away my job to people more capable than I am, I show them trust. Trusting others is not optional when leading large numbers of people. I'm not talking about hanging all of your laundry out every day for everyone to see. I'm talking about placing yourself into the hands of capable people you have in-fluenced over the years.

I remember early on during my first years at Timberline Church. (The church had been established sixty years before I came on the scene.) I came to a board meeting to discuss the need for a youth pastor. At that time, the entire church staff con-sisted of a secretary and myself. I planned to start by finding a way to budget for this new position. Our financial report for the month showed that we were $8,000 in the red. Our total monthly income at this time was about $15,000. I asked for in-put and counsel from these people whom God had placed around me. They began talking about the need and vision for young people in our church. I described the person I was con-sidering for the job. They were excited and filled with faith. I urged them to make it a matter of prayer over the next few months. I'll never forget when one of them spoke up and said, "We can't afford to wait that long." (Oh, for more deacons like that!) It caught me off-guard. They began to discuss the possi-bilities. I sat there with my eyes bulging out as I looked at the fi-nancial report and listened to Joshua and Caleb say, "We can do this." After a few minutes of synergy, one of them said, "Call him up and see when he can come." I sat there, dumbfounded. My heart rate jumped as I began to think about the conse-quences of this decision: "This is my first pastorate...we have no money for this...what if we go under...we are in the red." These thoughts rolled around in my mind for what seemed like a thou-sand years. Finally I said, "We're going to go around the room one at a time. I want each of you to respond with a 'yes' or a 'no.' I'll go last." Each person said "yes."

I was stuck—as much as I wanted to have the faith for this, I didn't. I didn't know the history of the church at that point. I didn't know the potential of these great people. But we secured a line of credit at the bank and asked for pledges from the congregation the following Sunday. I invited the youth pastor and he joined our team. The very next month, we were in the black. We've never been in the red since. We've never done that same thing the same way again either! I had to learn to trust the guidance of God coming through capable leaders in this fellowship. Leaders who do not trust will never themselves prove to be trustworthy.

Trust is a giant muscle that must be exercised daily in your life as well as in the life of the church. We receive great rewards when we trust others in ministry. We experience these great rewards when we team up with other Christians to accomplish spiritual tasks. Do you trust other people? If I asked you to talk to me about trust, would you tell me a story about a time you got burned or a story of a time you were blessed because you trusted another? When you trust capable people, you're opening the garage door for others to participate in the vision.

> **When you trust capable people, you're opening the garage door for others to participate in the vision.**

WILLINGNESS

Willingness is a condition of the heart. I've learned through the years that there are many things I must be willing to do in order to be effective as a Christian leader. Each of these things exposes something else in my personal garage. I'll give you a short list to get you thinking. I urge you to make your own list of things God is putting in your heart concerning your willingness.

Willingness to say "I'm sorry"

This simply means "I blew it!" I've had to say "I'm sorry" privately and publicly. I see many pastors who resist acknowledging that they are wrong even once. This is both unscriptural and unrealistic. People actually trust you more when they hear you say "I'm sorry" after you blow it than if they never hear you admit you've blown it! Hopefully you won't have to do this very often, or people won't trust you as a leader.

I remember when I was a youth pastor and I was asked to come to Fort Collins as a senior pastor. I went to my senior pastor and talked to him about the whole process. When I was planning my departure, I went to him with a pad of paper and a pen. I asked him to give me any counsel that would help me. I will never forget what he told me. He said I would need to do three things from the heart. "Oh boy," I thought. "This is gonna be profound." "First," he said, "you need to be able to do a good, meaningful wedding." I was thinking, "OK, fine—what's next?" "Second," he said, "you need to be able to do a good, meaningful funeral." I was really wondering at this point where the profound nuggets were. "Third," he said, "be sure you can say 'I'm sorry' and mean it." I remember writing these down and wondering if they would help me. Wow! Never did I realize just how simple and yet how profound these three things were. Weddings and funerals eventually impact every person in the church. And saying "I'm sorry" has been necessary many times because of all the simple mistakes I've made. When we learn from our mistakes, we build confidence in our followers. When you admit you're wrong, you open the garage door wide for others to help you clean up the mess.

> **❝ When you admit you're wrong, you open the garage door wide for others to help you clean up the mess. ❞**

Willingness to share success

I know how it feels when good things happen in our church and others want to give me the credit for it. Many times in my ministry, I've been praised for things in our church that I knew nothing about until after the fact. It's very humbling to look at someone and say, "Thank you for the compliment, but I didn't even know about that." When you share the success with others, you are in fact opening the garage door to those who are willing to work.

Willingness to accept responsibility— "the buck stops here"

There are many things I enjoy about the pastorate and some things I don't enjoy at all. However, I must accept the responsibility to do them both as well as I can. In this way, I'll be effective in letting people see my garage. At times, this means that I have to accept responsibility for a mistake made by someone I delegated to. When you accept your responsibility appropriately, you open the garage door for people to trust.

Willingness to be accountable

I've found accountability essential for leading people openly. I don't want to be viewed as the boss who calls all the shots. I'd much rather be the leader who knows when to pass to the open man who can make the shot. That means a win for everyone. Accountability means that I will practice discipline in my life. It means that I will live by the same code I expect those who are following me to live by. It means that I will not be the exception to the rule. It means our bookkeeper can ask me for a missing receipt without fear that I will be offended. It means the high road is a way of life and a journey filled with healthy memories. It also means that as I look back over the trail I have traveled, I will be able to say to others, "Follow me as I follow Christ." When you live in accountability to others, you open the garage door for them to cultivate accountability in their lives.

Willingness to give it away

I've found that someone else could do almost anything I do as a senior pastor. I want to remain faithful to the church and the city to which I have been called, as long as I can be effective in the Kingdom of God. When the day comes that God asks me to give it away, I want to be willing in my heart to give it away to those whom God has called. This kind of attitude really helps shape my day-to-day thought processes. I am able to think and dream about releasing ground we have gained to capable and trained leaders. Then I can put my efforts into claiming new ground. When I give the ministry away, it keeps me from falling into the trap of doing only what I'm comfortable doing. About the time I get comfortable with a certain role, I give it to someone who can take it to new heights. This releases me to move on to uncharted waters.

> 66 When you're willing to give meaningful ministry away to qualified and capable leaders, you're opening the garage door wide enough to make room for talented people. 99

I guarantee you that when these leadership qualities are lived out in your life, two things will happen:

1. People will know what they like about you.

2. People will know what they don't like about you.

Wow! Profound, isn't it? The rocket scientist in me comes out every now and then! The amazing thing about this is that you can lead people with greater confidence because you're not working so hard to meet their expectations. They love you for who you are—that's it! When you're willing to give meaningful ministry away to qualified and capable leaders, you're opening the garage door wide enough to make room for talented people.

Garage-Door Openers

1. List some of the differences between an "image-driven" front-door church and an open-garage-door church.

2. Why do you suppose it's difficult for us as church leaders and pastors to expose some of the weaknesses in our church?

3. What "atmosphere" exists in the church you lead? Is this intentional or by default? How can you improve it?

4. How do you model vulnerability and transparency in your life?

5. List some of the hindrances that may keep you from trusting others.

6. List two or three ministries that you have given away in the last year.

7. Pray that God will help you to open the garage door of your own life as you attempt to open the garage door of the church you lead. Complete this sentence: "Lord, help me to be more willing to…"

Chapter 2

The Shelving in the Garage:

ORGANIZING FOR GROWTH

One of the great things about some garages is their organizational structure. I love visiting those garages that have everything you need close by; the kinds of garages that make you want to sit and find something to work on. This kind of garage is rare and requires time and energy to organize. Generally speaking, most of us have garages that have a few shelves thrown together. These shelves are overloaded and overburdened to the point of sagging and almost breaking.

Unfortunately, the structure of our churches often reflects this sagging image. We're guilty of overloading the shelves because of our rush to set down the weight. We need to repair this in order to be effective.

Just the other day, I unloaded a bunch of stuff in the garage for work on a new room we're adding downstairs, including nails, Sheetrock mud, screws, trim, and sacks of hardware. I had stuff everywhere on those shelves. When I actually started working on that room downstairs, I couldn't find anything I needed without cleaning off the whole shelf. I believe this is precisely what's happening in our churches. We've become scattered doing so many things that we often haven't taken the time to clear off the old before starting the new.

> **"** Organization puts healthy shelves and benches in place to help us accomplish the tasks that we need to finish in the local church. **"**

Organization puts healthy shelves and benches in place to help us accomplish the tasks that we need to finish in the local church.

We need to view structure as a necessary component of effective and productive work. As pastors and leaders, we all sometimes get frustrated with the forms and paperwork that must be filled out. I remember when I could just ask for a check or set a date for an activity without any "red tape." Through the years I've learned some valuable lessons about shelving and organization. I've summarized those lessons in the following acrostic:

S—Space

Every garage has a certain amount of space in it. I realize that it never seems to be enough. The bigger you build it, the more you put in it. I don't know too many homeowners who say, "This garage is just too big." The leadership style you possess can be viewed as space. How much do you need? What are the things that tie you up and what are the things that make you feel free? Some leaders are very specific and organized with the space issue. Other great leaders are more hands-off and carefree. It's not as important to organize a certain way as it is to understand the way you must organize in order to fit who you are.

Another leadership aspect of space is the schedule that you keep on a daily basis. When you start stacking everything up on a shelf rather than acting upon it, you lose your space. It's that simple. When you lose your space, you begin to feel overwhelmed, and you won't even have the energy to begin. I can always tell when I've started to lose my space—I get frustrated, and I want to withdraw. I won't finish tasks or start new ones. Guess what? When this happens, I lose heart for everything except escaping. Escaping only compounds the problem because new stuff is always being added to the shelf. I highly recommend that you go through the stuff on your shelf (or desk) using the following rule:

• *Make a commitment to handle each item or piece of mail only once. It should be placed in one of three places:*

The trash can. We all receive a lot of "almost-junk mail" mail. I used to set it aside, thinking I would respond to it later. That was a mistake. Waiting to respond later only took away my space. If it's going to go into the trash can later, it can go into the trash can now. Don't keep those articles and flyers around unless you know why you want to keep them. The trash can serves you well because it allows you the freedom to decide, right now, whether you'll ever need an item again.

The "to do" file. This isn't a collect-all file that gets disorganized and fat. This file is reserved for the items you know you'll need to respond to either today or within a few days. If you start doing any of these tasks right away, you won't get your shelf cleared off. Too often we make the call or write the letter before we've cleared off the shelf. This is a mistake because it keeps us from proper priorities. Go through everything before responding to anything. I keep a black file-folder in my left-hand drawer. I set it out on the corner of my desk each morning and place things in it throughout the day that need action. I'll typically work through that file before lunch and before going home. This file includes phone calls that need to be returned, letters that need to be written, thank-you notes, and other details. I like the simple question "How do you make a small job big?" The answer? "Put it off." Learn to keep the shelf clean by acting quickly.

The right person. Many of the things you look at need attention. Learn to decide quickly whether something needs your response or if someone else could respond to it, and decide quickly who you will give these tasks to. When you give away the right things to the right people, the shelf remains clear and useful.

> 66 Make sure your shelf has only the things on it that need to be there. 99

Space is an important concept for your consideration. Work smart, and stay organized. Don't fall into the trap of refusing to act now. Make sure your shelf has only the things on it that need to be there.

Take a moment to look over your space.

H—Help

Pastors always need help. The garage shelf is a great help. It takes care of things you need to release. You can trust the shelf to store things for you until you return to them. This is what good help does for a gifted leader. It keeps things, balances things, accepts things, and stores things that the leader needs to keep around, just in case. The shelf can become a real help to you when it's used properly. Consider certain people that you need in your life to become the shelving system in your garage:

YOUR SPOUSE

The greatest helper a married spiritual leader has is his or her spouse. Your spouse is like a shelf upon which you can place your most valued possessions. He or she is the protector, the keeper, and the security for all of those things you must set down from time to time. Your spouse watches over things like:

Self-Doubt

If you've ever wondered what in the world you're doing in your leadership role, you should feel right at home. We all have times we're overwhelmed with our responsibilities. Laying my weakness and frailties on the shelf of my spouse is a great help! Her understanding and support are truly a help-shelf that sustains me when nothing else can.

Early in our marriage, we would often get into arguments right before I was going to speak or lead a meeting. This was a devastating dilemma. The weight created by conflict such as this could bend the shelf and eventually break it. It caused me to carry the weight alone. I began to feel my insecurities rise up and bring that nagging self-doubt back to my mind. When I entered those meetings with sagging shelves, they became real thorns that would "stick" me every time I wanted to make a difference.

When we realized what we were doing, my wife and I began to repair the support shelf that we needed to be for one another. We quickly learned the power of that shelf. As we supported and helped each other, we were able to reach our potential as God enabled us. My self-doubt faded away as that spouse shelf remained strong and useful in times of struggle.

Temptation

Your spouse is the one who can help you overcome areas in your life that can destroy you if they're not dealt with. He or she knows you better than anyone and needs to know you even better. You and your spouse must work hard to build a protective shield around each other so that you will be able to lay temptation down on the shelf with confidence and security. I'm not suggesting that you call home every time you are tempted by something, but rather that you open your life to a place of reliance on your helper. Do you remember the Genesis account?

"So the man gave names to all the livestock, the birds of the air and all the beasts of the field. But for Adam no suitable helper was found. So the Lord God caused the man to fall into a deep sleep; and while he was sleeping, he took one of the man's ribs and closed up the place with flesh. Then the Lord God made a woman from the rib he had taken out of the man, and he brought her to the man. The man said, 'This is now bone of my bones and flesh of my flesh; she shall be called "woman," for she was taken out of man' " (Genesis 2:20-23).

God's intention was to create a union so strong that it would ease the stress of life. In this passage, God demonstrated that we all need a place to set down the heavy load. God has blessed each of us with a helper to afford us this privilege. I realize that many issues of temptation are appropriate to share with other accountability partners. However, I resist the trend to depend on other sources more than on my own helpmate from God. She is an incredible strength that allows me to place temptation on the shelf for careful review.

Disappointments

When I come home and have the opportunity to lay my disappointments on the shelf, I feel revived and refreshed. Just talking about that meeting, sermon, confrontation, employee, or financial challenge brings me to a place of rest. Once I lay it on the shelf, I feel a new freedom.

Anger

Anger is the silent thief of energy that creeps in when you least expect it. It comes into the soul of a spiritual leader without warning. I remember being in a church service once when the pastor was preaching and the sound man was messing with the sound. It was distracting. However, when the pastor began to verbally pound on this guy, I was completely stunned. The anger that came from this pastor was so sharp and quick that he lost all credibility with the attendees for the remaining points of his message. I wondered what had happened to this man to make him so short-fused and angry. An unchurched person would have been blown away and may never have returned.

I must choose to bring my anger to my wife for counsel. When I share what it is that makes me angry, she is willing to share in my anger and help me find a solution. The practice of sharing these kinds of things with your spouse must be entered into carefully. The temperament of your spouse may be such that you need to be very careful about what you share. The point is, you need to be willing to get your anger out on the table so that you'll be able to move through the challenges you face.

Financial Struggles

There are two points I want to make about finances. The first has to do with the finances of your home. It doesn't really matter who the check writer is in your family; you need to build a strong shelf of communication to help minimize the stress of financial decisions. Pastors and their families are often struggling financially and no one is talking about it. Deal honestly and openly with this issue so you'll be strong enough to tackle the budget issues of the church.

The second point is in regard to the finances of the church. My wife knows very little about our church budget. It's never been important to me that she has a full understanding of all these matters. What does matter is that she has allowed me many times to lay this burden on the shelf for relief. She listens and tries to feel the weight of it without trying to solve it. After all, I don't want her to solve it; I only want to set this burden down somewhere for a moment so that I can rest. The help shelf is cleared for me to lay things down for temporary relief.

People

Once a non-pastor friend asked me if people ever stressed me out. I jumped all over his question so fast that it frightened him. The expression on my face said more than words could have ever said. I gave him that "You've got to be kidding" look and said, "People are the pain of my life, the thorn in my side, the nightmares of my night." I really don't feel this way about people all the time, but at that particular time I was fighting everything and everybody. I was frustrated with staff, with deacons, with leaders, with sound people, and with secretaries. I shocked myself by what I said and came to the realization that I was probably the biggest problem of all.

When I shared with my wife some of my hurts and challenges it really helped to clean up my attitude. The worst thing you can do with this kind of attitude is to hold it in. The appropriate shelf to lay this kind of attitude on is your spouse.

YOUR SECRETARY

I tell you with confidence that a secretary will make or break a pastor. As your spouse helps with the personal and private issues of your life, your secretary serves as your business and professional shelf. I've been blessed with great people who help me in the ministry, and I know that I wouldn't have survived without their support. The secretary shelf enables me to organize my work and relationships in ways that fit my style of ministry. As you organize your garage, make certain that this shelf is built solidly and durably enough to last a long time. Your secretary needs to have traits that enable him or her to be strong enough for you to lay down the load once in a while.

My secretary should:

Know me. I must help with this process by being open and honest. It's been a real joy of mine to work long enough with the same people to develop meaningful relationships. When I allow my secretaries the opportunity to see inside my world and know me personally, it gives them the opportunity to strengthen and encourage me with the support I need from that shelf. One of my goals in the ministry is to make certain that those people who work with me on a daily basis really know me and that I really know them. Obviously, these relationships must stay pure and holy at all times. I'm not talking about sharing my struggles and temptations as I would share with my wife; I'm referring to staff members' understanding about how I think and how I act.

Trust me. I must give proof of my trustworthiness by returning phone calls, being on time, giving advance notice, living with integrity, and never gossiping about people. I must be where I say I'll be and do what I say I'll do. If I do these little things well, I'll earn the trust of this important person. Secretaries must trust me so that they can accomplish their work. I may not always be able to share details about letters they type or phone calls they receive. Trust allows them to work freely and openly. It allows them to ask the questions they need to ask without crossing that line into breaking a confidence. If they've developed that trust, it will be easy for them to follow me.

Care. A secretary should care about my family, my friends, my interests, my whole life, and me. This can be cultivated through time and experience. This may seem a bit selfish. However, the reality is that if they don't care, they won't serve as a shelf that enables me to be at my best. When I function at my best, others can reach their potential as well. Please use the exercise at the end of this chapter to explore some of these important concepts.

Work. There's nothing worse than putting something really valuable on a shelf and having the shelf collapse. A secretary must be able to accept and handle the pressure that comes with the job. The work a secretary does is a tremendous help only if he or she holds up under the weight of big issues.

My secretary or associate pastor could make most of the decisions that come across my desk. They all know my heart well enough to represent me well. I have great expectations that the work will be done and that assignments will be followed through on. I must trust these people so that I don't have to check up on the tasks they are assigned to do.

Be gentle...and tough as nails. Ha! I'm sure my secretary will love that line. This is a gift that your assistant needs to have. It's that wonderful, rare ability to direct people to the right source without making them feel unwanted, unneeded, or rejected. Everybody wants to see *you*! This is impossible and must be handled with great care. Your secretary must be a reflection of you. Much of this is decided by the size of the congregation you lead or by the gifts you have. If you are leading a smaller church, you may want to handle every call that comes in. This allows you to be informed quickly. The downside of taking every call is that the day may come when the church reaches a size that keeps you from this task. People can become so attached to "you" that growth will never be successful.

Strive for excellence. There's something wonderful and encouraging to me about knowing that any job done through my secretaries will be excellent. Finding ways to make things better is a critical trait that they should possess.

This shelf is powerful in the long haul. It changes the organization and causes it to improve. In a day and age of change, not all changes are good. But many of the technological advancements in our culture have enabled us to do the job better, more quickly, and more efficiently than ever before.

YOUR PASTORAL TEAM

I'm quite aware that not everyone is privileged to work in a setting with other pastors and staff. Those of you who don't have help in these areas are truly the heroes of the local church. You do it all. Wow! My prayer for you is that you'll be able to grow with the church you lead and will experience the growth that justifies and requires additional help.

Your pastoral team needs to have three qualities:

Character. Integrity is the big issue. If the character of godliness is built into their lives, you'll have little worry about their job performance. Be thorough and check references as you build your staff. Turn over every rock necessary to discover the character of each person. Character is the quality that allows you to lay the load you have onto the shelf and know it will be safe there.

Calling. I'm not very hung up on knowing the time or moment when someone felt "called" into the ministry. I believe all of us are called into a ministry. I'm referring more to a specific desire to be in the setting we're in, a passion for our style of ministry. I want those working with me to understand why we're doing the things we're doing. It's not enough to just show up and do a job. "Calling" allows a person the inside strength and fortitude necessary to hold up under pressure.

Excellence. It's obviously important that they have a measure of ability. Even if they need to be trained and equipped, there must be potential. I believe we need to expect excellence. I've learned that excellence is a trait that can be developed and nurtured in people. Give people on your team the opportunity to expand their abilities. We're fortunate to live in an era of incredible helps. Conferences, tapes, seminars, and books can all be used to help these great people reach their potential.

YOUR CHURCH LEADERS

Each church functions a bit differently. Deacons or elders lead some churches while pastors or congregations lead others. Many churches are led by some combination of the above. I can't imagine life without my deacons. I hope they can't imagine life without me!

The church-leader shelf is of great value to the pastor. I view this shelf as one of my greatest "helps." These are people who have come alongside me and our pastoral teams to support, pray for, and help accomplish the vision of our church. We meet monthly, and once each quarter we invite all the pastors and deacons and their spouses to come together for a meal and a time of connection. We pray together, play together, laugh together, and share our lives with one another. This is a shelf very few pastors take the time to properly access. The church-leader shelf is a shelf that helps me by being honest and open to new ideas and concepts. My deacons are a tremendous springboard to launch new ministries and outreaches.

E—Energy

Today I'm writing from Tiberas, Israel, the site of the feeding of the five thousand. Remember? Jesus took the disciples and taught thousands of people while they were seated on the hillside. The Bible tells us that they became hungry. Christ used this common need to teach a very valuable lesson to his disciples. As the disciples sensed the hunger of the crowd, they could only think of one answer. They said, "Send them away." Jesus said, "Build a new shelf"...that's my paraphrase!

The disciples were forced to organize the mess in the garage. Christ told the disciples to seat the people in groups. Proper organizational structure is perhaps the most commonly missing element in churches today. It keeps churches from maintaining energy to accomplish the miracles that God wants to accomplish through them. Jesus was constantly trying to empower his disciples to build new shelves. It was difficult for them—all they saw was a bigger mess.

I used to think about what it would be like to pastor a big church. When our church attendance was 150, we were always looking for teachers, workers, and ushers. I remember thinking that if we could just get another one hundred people or so, we would have the help we needed. As we began to grow, I quickly learned that more people only create more messes. Church growth with new members is extremely messy. The energy level of the church is dependent upon proper shelving to organize what God is doing. Energy drains from the church when we have no structure to maintain the organization. A church wanting to open the garage door for all to come in must have a structure that allows the growth to be organized. If a semi truck pulled up in front of your house with tools, lumber, and equipment, and you couldn't get it organized, you wouldn't be able to tap the potential of the materials.

Church energy is a strange and intriguing phenomenon. It's necessary to maintain this energy through seasons of growth. A church that doesn't organize and make adjustments to the shelving needs won't maintain growth.

We're all familiar with the term "the back door." The back door is directly related to the organization/shelving issue we're talking about. Many times when we haven't maintained our growth, we discover the problem is related to this very issue.

Ask some hard questions about your church and its shelving. Are these shelves securely in place to keep "big mo" (momentum) going? Many churches have grown to a certain level and cannot seem to grow beyond it. I'm convinced the solution is usually something simpler than we'd like to admit. We typically try to fix the problem by repeating the same things we've tried before. Take some time right now to think through structural issues that may be quelling the growth of the church. Ask God to reveal these things to you and be willing to add another shelf or two.

L—Lift

The word "shelf" implies lift. Most shelves are designed to lift things up and keep them in or out of sight. This lift provides easy access. The Bible says something very interesting about "lift." "But I, when I am lifted up from the earth, will draw all men to myself" (John 12:32).

How do you suppose shelving or organization in the church can lift up the name of Christ? Let's look at three ways:

1. It creates a picture people can see. When the church has a clear structure that people can see, it brings them understanding and trust. We live in a day when few people are trusted for anything. We don't give our trust away easily. It takes time, knowledge, and understanding. If people find out that the pastor takes the offering home after each service and counts it alone, trust will be violated. The pastor may be honest, but that shelf is broken. That shelf doesn't lift up the integrity of the church. It actually tears it down. Shelves and safeguards that lift the integrity of the church must remain above reproach. Proper shelves lift up the structure so that people can quickly assess it and determine whether they want to be a part.

2. It maximizes space. Proper shelves allow you to be a good steward of what God has given you. We currently have five weekend services. It's not my first choice. It's grueling, but it's what we must do. We've used every square inch of our facility to accomplish the vision God has put in our hearts. We're currently working on a major relocation project. We'll get to go back to three weekend services when phase one is finished. I grow weary of people who complain about their facilities when they haven't really tapped them. Build some good organizational shelves!

3. It allows you to focus on the need. When my garage is clean and things are put in their proper spots, I can focus clearly on the challenge at hand. The mess in the corner or the clutter on my bench won't distract me. I'll focus on the issue at hand and clearly see it. Many pastors have good intentions to fix a problem, but getting to it uncovers three others. This creates frustration and anxiety.

As leaders we need to focus on the issues that God wants us to focus on. I was reminded of this the other day when I made a visit to a hospital emergency room. It was spotless. The beds were ready for the need. People were prepared and the equipment was waiting.

When the broken and wounded came in, the staff didn't need to wade through a lot of red tape to get the job done. They were focused and efficient. Are we ready for the wounded and needy?

V—Visibility

In the previous section, we focused on our ability to see the need. The visibility issue is another important reason to have a good shelving system. If you build good shelves, you'll be able to find what you need when you need it. It's truly a wonderful thing to walk into that perfect garage that has everything in place just waiting to be used. Many times I've needed something that I knew I had, but I couldn't find it. I remember when we built the house we live in now. We bought a small two-bedroom mobile home to live in while we built it, and five of us moved in. Fun! Yeah, right! I remember the Saturday we moved in. (Big mistake!) I got up to go to church on Sunday and couldn't find my dress shoes. I knew I had them, but I didn't know where they were. I finally found them and sighed that sweet sigh of relief.

We need to have shelving and organization in our churches so that we will be able to see where things are, to evaluate them effectively, and to make decisions based on a true understanding of the facts.

> 66 We need to have shelving and organization in our churches so that we will be able to see where things are, to evaluate them effectively, and to make decisions based on a true understanding of the facts. 99

I—Interests

Many garages have shelving organized by interests. You can walk through the garage and see the sections of shelves that contain items which all relate to one another. Here in Colorado, it's typical for people to have camping sections in their garages. All of the camping gear is neatly stacked and piled. This allows the owner to find specific items quickly and use them regularly.

The "interests" shelves of a church are unique. I believe that God often calls a church and provides a specific strength that might not be found in another church in that community. The "interests" shelves in your church should be clearly defined and marked. Take a moment right now to list the things your church does with greater detail and care than another. What is that special calling you have that not every church has? This is not to create competition, but rather to give you clear direction about utilizing this strength for the kingdom of God. Just as each of us has certain gifts and abilities that God has placed in our lives, God has raised up church bodies with certain strengths and interests to reach our world. Do you remember the seven churches in Revelation? Each of those bodies had interests and abilities as well as weaknesses and challenges. It's your job to begin to organize the church you lead in such a way that you can do this unique thing effectively and with confidence. Accept the special mantle upon your church and fulfill your mission. Look at the following list and rate the interests and the effectiveness of the ministries in the church you lead.

> **66** When you're able to articulate the interests of your church and organize according to your strengths, you'll begin to open the garage door to your community. **99**

Drama	1	2	3	4	5	6	7	8	9	10
Worship	1	2	3	4	5	6	7	8	9	10
Teaching	1	2	3	4	5	6	7	8	9	10
Preaching	1	2	3	4	5	6	7	8	9	10
Evangelism	1	2	3	4	5	6	7	8	9	10
Discipleship	1	2	3	4	5	6	7	8	9	10
Big Events	1	2	3	4	5	6	7	8	9	10
Small Groups	1	2	3	4	5	6	7	8	9	10
Service	1	2	3	4	5	6	7	8	9	10
Prayer	1	2	3	4	5	6	7	8	9	10
Others:										

When you're able to articulate the interests of your church and organize according to your strengths, you'll begin to open the garage door to your community.

Your community will see you at your best as you achieve specific goals.

N—Necessities

Every good garage has a place for necessities, those items you just can't live without. I'm certain that the list of necessities would vary from person to person. For me it's nails, hammers, pliers, and wrenches.

The bottom line for the church is that we all must do the basics well. I would challenge you to list the items you would call the basics of your church. Then ask the haunting question: "Is our church structured in such a way that we can accomplish all of the basics without organizational confusion or in-house fighting?" Often, when I've had the privilege to work with churches, I've discovered that the list of basics they came up with created real tension when compared to the structure they embraced. For instance, if you listed small groups as a necessity for your church but operated with a structure that gave priority and budget to big events, you'd be frustrated all year long. You'd be unable to recruit, train, and develop small-group leaders because you wouldn't have the money necessary for success. We must learn to budget and establish our church structure so that the basics are the priority.

> **"** We must learn to budget and establish our church structure so that the basics are the priority. **"**

I have a friend who collects old cars. His necessity is his heated garage for the old cars. His new Cadillac sits outside. He has strategically made the space for these old cars a priority. I believe we must make the shelving in our churches serve our priorities and our call. This is why each church will look different from another. We all have different opinions on the basics. Our church budgets vary greatly on things like printing, mailings, furnishings, parking, sound systems, lighting, media centers, and so on. It's because our necessary basics vary. We must determine our structure and organize our shelving around our desire to implement our basics.

G—Gifts

Organize the garage in such a way that each item has a specific place to be stored and utilized. Most garage organizers don't build one big gigantic shelf in the garage for everything to be stacked on. Rather, they build the shelves according to the needs. A woodworker would place a higher emphasis on certain organizational

> 66 Opening the garage door for all to see requires you to assess the giftedness of your church. 99

needs than an auto mechanic would. In the same way, we need to examine the gifts within our churches in order to build the appropriate shelves.

Opening the garage door for all to see requires you to assess the giftedness of your church. To begin, check out 1 Corinthians 12.

We must make a commitment to build the shelves of the garage in such a way that they can contain all of these gifts. If we build only one big shelf and try to stack everything on it, we will be confused and frustrated. I remember going into my garage and seeing a shelf that was a catchall kind of shelf. It was very large and overloaded. It was sagging in the middle, and it needed to be strengthened. If I couldn't find what I was looking for in the garage, I would resort to that shelf. Slowly and carefully, I would begin removing everything so that I could see under, over, and behind. It took strength and energy just to look. Often as I was looking for an item, I would get sidetracked by another item I'd been looking for the week before. "Wow, here it is. I may need this later," I would say as I set the item aside on a new cluttered shelf. Often I would forget what it was I needed so badly. If I never found what I was looking for on that big shelf, I was really in trouble because of the bigger mess I had just created. Does this sound remotely familiar in ministry? We strive to shore up a certain ministry and discover five more needs that need to be shored up in a different ministry. Rearranging the clutter creates absolutely no change in effectiveness.

Regardless of your denomination or background, you must come to a decision about how you'll utilize the giftedness of the church that you lead. You don't use every tool in the garage for every project. So it becomes important to organize and place these gifts in places where you can find them when they're needed.

Here are some suggestions to maximize your use of the gifts represented in your church. Make a list of six or seven basic things you want to know about your church each week. My list included income and tithe, attendance, next weekend's special music, the spotlight (a special missions or informational four-minute moment during each service), hospital visitation information, next weekend's worship team, and the order of the service.

Then make another list of things you want to know on a monthly basis. This list might include things like a small-group report, a discipleship-training report, a first-time guest report, church trends, parking issues, and a financial report. Make a third list of things you want to know on a quarterly basis. This list might include department reports, staff pastors' reports, and a goal-achievement report. Make sure these lists provide you with what you need to feel informed about the direction of your preaching, teaching, and vision-casting.

> 66 Build shelves to contain certain gifts that can be tapped quickly and easily to stay ahead of a potential collapse. 99

Having access to this information could be essential for making directional changes for the church before the shelf is sagging to the point of breaking. Remember, when the big shelf breaks, you really have a mess on your hands. Keep people around you who can assess these things quickly. Work smarter, not harder. Build shelves to contain certain gifts that can be tapped quickly and easily to stay ahead of a potential collapse.

S —Space

H —Help

E —Energy

L —Lift

V —Visibility

I —Interests

N —Necessities

G —Gifts

Garage-Door Openers

1. List the areas of administration that are wearing you down. Discuss this list with others who can help you prioritize these items.

2. List two or three qualities that you really appreciate about your spouse. Determine now that you will express your thoughts to him or her this week.

3. How could you better communicate your needs to those with whom you work closely? Do they know your struggles? Do they support you and give you a shelf to utilize?

4. Evaluate the purpose of all meetings at your church. Are there any that you could eliminate or shorten?

5. Describe the relationship you would like to cultivate with your church leaders. Discuss how you might develop that kind of relationship with them.

6. What are some of the reporting tools that you need to create in order to be well-informed?

7. Have you placed enough shelving or too much shelving in your garage? List some changes you need to make in the shelving.

Chapter **3**

The Workbench:
INITIATING CHANGE

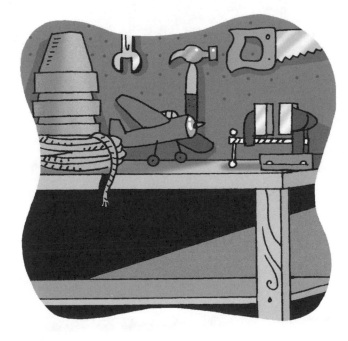

If you're like me, you've got a workbench in your garage. We call them workbenches, but they're usually places to pile things we don't want to put away. The workbench collects things like tools, plants, wires, furniture, rope, dirt, hobby stuff, and toys. It's useful, and it serves the garage well.

When the workbench is used properly, miracles happen and change occurs. Just the other day, I used my workbench to fix a little knob from the door of our entertainment center that had split open. I placed some glue inside it and squeezed it together with the vice on the corner of my workbench. The vice held it in place until the glue set; now it's like new.

The workbench is an essential item in the church. It's where we focus our energy to accomplish certain tasks. It represents our projects and priorities. It's the place where we initiate change. Tragically, we church leaders often pile projects on our workbenches and then get caught up in life, work, family, and everything else that we're trying to balance. The broken items remain broken.

Jesus took note of issues that created dysfunction. One day he walked into the Temple and became keenly aware of the need for the workbench. He found all he needed to make a whip to drive the moneychangers out of the Temple. He walked into a situation of selling, overpricing, and deception and immediately went to work. When he said, "My house will be called a house of prayer," he meant it! How many other religious people walked by those same moneychangers and didn't do a thing about it? How many spiritual leaders walk through the church today and see no need to place anything on the workbench?

What are the primary purpose and goal of your church? People like George Barna, Bill Hybels, Rick Warren, John Maxwell, and others have challenged us to ask and answer this question. We fail to be effective in completing small tasks because we haven't taken the time to think through our priorities. Once you have the purpose question answered, you'll be able to start working toward the goal. You'll be able to overcome the temptation to resign and leave the church, and the frustration over idealistic expectations. You can begin to work on some simple concepts.

Start by taking a look at five main priorities of the church: worship, fellowship, discipleship, evangelism, and ministry. Let's step back from our ministry for a moment and be honest about how our churches are broken in each of these areas. Then let's place each of the broken items on the workbench and repair them.

Worship: Expressing Worth to God

REPAIR I: WORSHIP IN SPIRIT AND TRUTH.

One of the greatest challenges we face as pastors and church leaders is worship style. The problem is that we forget what real worship is: a way to praise and honor God.

In John 4:24, Jesus makes a profound statement about worship:

"God is spirit, and his worshipers must worship in spirit and in truth."

What does it mean for us to worship God in "spirit" or "pneuma" (the Greek word for spirit)? Pneuma is a current of air, a breath, or a breeze. Worship in pneuma means to enter a realm of deep emotional satisfaction and refreshment during our expression of love to God. It's a moment of serenity that enables people to face the issues of life with the confidence that God is breathing with them and in them.

> 66 We need to provide an opportunity for people to sense the wind of God cleansing its way through their shattered dreams and broken spirits. 99

The people who fill our churches have tremendous emotional needs. Their days are full of pressures and demands that deplete their emotional strength. The woman Jesus spoke to in John 4 was not unlike people in our own day. She had experienced life with five different husbands and was living with a man who was not her husband. Think of the hurt, pain, confusion, hardness, brokenness, and emotional struggles she faced daily. These are the challenges of our generation as well. We need to provide an opportunity for people to sense the wind of God cleansing its way through their shattered dreams and broken spirits.

This can happen through a variety of worship styles. Style simply helps worshippers relax and become involved during the worship experience. People often get tense during worship if they don't know the words or the guitar is screaming. Some prefer the organ, others prefer a full band, while still others prefer country music. All of these styles must submit to the ultimate goal: to sense, taste, feel, and commit to a fresh burst of God's wind filling the sail of a stagnant life. Once that sail is full, our journey with God becomes a reality.

Pneuma is more than a meaningless corporate shout or an orchestrated tear from the eye. It's a deep sense of vitality springing up from the depth of a hungry soul. It's that moment in which God makes a deposit into people's weary lives and hope is born anew. In worship, God captures us; we don't capture him.

What does it mean to worship God in "truth" or "aletheia" (the Greek word for truth)? Aletheia is "verity, forthrightness, and honesty. Nothing hidden." Jesus wants us to worship in pneuma and in aletheia together. To worship in pneuma is to be compelled by this burst of fresh wind to worship in truth and to live with integrity. Aletheia is about how we live our lives. The woman at the well experienced an incredible life change. The people of her community couldn't believe she changed so drastically. This is an example of what happens when we experience aletheia. We begin to discover the truth and change our lives to merge with it.

How can we incorporate these principles of worship into the lifeblood of the churches we lead? How can we put our churches on the workbench and repair them so that we're teaching others to worship in spirit (pneuma) and truth (aletheia)?

First, start by looking at where you are personally. Are you truly worshipping God in spirit and in truth? It's easy to get so caught up in the order and details of the church service that we don't model for others what it looks like to worship. Are you fresh? Is your sail full? Is there a sense of spiritual refreshment in your life? Are you walking in truth? Church leaders often focus so much on providing these opportunities for others that they themselves are depleted of spiritual health as it relates to worship.

Second, look closely at the worship experience of the church you lead. Shine the workbench light on it and examine it carefully. Turn it sideways and upside down; view it from many angles. As you do this, ask God to reveal truth to you. Ask yourself these questions:

• Are there power struggles related to the worship experience?

• Is our worship carefully planned?

• Are the teams leading the church in worship walking in unity?

Here are some suggestions to improve your worship celebration.

• Provide the lyrics for those who don't know them. You could project them onto a screen or include a lyrics handout in the church bulletin.

• Make certain the instruments are a complement to the service rather than a distraction. Strive for excellence in your music ministry.

• Instruct people about the value of the moment and invite them to join in. Don't just run through the elements of your worship service. Talk to your congregation; explain what you are doing and why. Be a worship leader, not a worship facilitator.

• Talk about the theme of the worship service. Help people get the point of your service. Read Scripture related to the theme. Have people give testimonies related to the theme. Do all you can to reinforce the main point.

REPAIR 2: DON'T SPIRITUALIZE PREFERENCES AND STYLES.

We must teach the difference between a mandated absolute and a personal preference. I often ask people each to look at the shoes on the person next to them. Then I say, "Aren't you glad you don't have to wear those shoes?" Some people like styles that others may not care for. Music is no different. Styles and sounds change with time. What used to be unacceptable to some is now commonplace. What used to be commonplace is now unacceptable to some. We must encourage people not to get hung up on style.

We recently talked about preferences in a fun way during our weekend services. I asked John Lawson, our Performing Arts Pastor, to get a band together that could illustrate this point. In the middle of my sermon on worship, I stopped and asked these musicians to come to the platform. I told the congregation that we were going to vote on the kind of music that was best for worshipping God. The band played the first verse of the great hymn "Amazing Grace" in several different musical styles.

The first time they played it with the organ. John even put on a white English wig. It was fun! People loved it and applauded. I asked how many of them thought this was the style that honored God, and many hands went up.

Then the band put on cowboy hats and filled the house with the twang of "Amazing Grace" in country western style. To my surprise, the place went crazy. I then asked how many people preferred this style. The house exploded with applause and "yee-ha's."

> **66** We must release people to enjoy a variety of styles in worship and teach them to worship God, not a style. **99**

Then the band played the song once again, this time in rock 'n' roll style. The guitarist took off in a Jimi Hendrix-style solo. People once again cheered and applauded with joy.

I asked the question, "How can we get along if we like these different styles?" I then suggested that God is calling all people to his throne room to *worship*, not to worship in a certain style nor to judge others on the basis of their worship preferences. We must release people to enjoy a variety of styles in worship and teach them to worship God, not a style.

REPAIR 3: USE MORE VARIETY IN YOUR EXPRESSION OF WORSHIP.

We've allowed the world to take away many great forms of expression. Don't be afraid to use instruments, readings, drama, Scripture, artwork, banners, silence, clapping, laughter, shouting, kneeling, darkness, or candles in worship. We need to take these art forms back and release people to experience greater variety in their expressions of worship to God. The basis for this approach is found in the book of Psalms where meditation, silence, writing, painting, singing, banners, and other worship expressions are described.

REPAIR 4: PRAISE OTHER CHURCHES WITH DIFFERENT WORSHIP STYLES.

It will do wonders for your congregation if you say something nice about the church across town. We give all of our pastors a weekend off each quarter because of the numerous responsibilities they have each weekend. This is a weekend to go to a different church if they so choose. It's not vacation time; it's simply a time of refreshment amidst a busy church scene.

On my weekends off, I often go to other churches in our area. It's not uncommon for me to share with our congregation something I learned from that church. I take great delight in naming the pastor and the church I attended and how blessed I was by the presence of God in those people. Whenever I do this, I always sense the smile of God. The people appreciate viewing God's kingdom as much bigger than any one church.

The bottom line is, we need to help people discover how to worship God. To do that, we need to give worship ample time and emphasis in our services. Sometimes it's difficult to fit everything in, but we must plan effectively and do our best to encourage people to worship.

Fellowship: Connecting Through Community

REPAIR 1: MAKE RELATIONSHIPS IMPORTANT.

We're not thinking small enough—small groups, that is. When our church was smaller, we struggled to keep people because we couldn't provide all the ministries they wanted. The phone calls went like this:

"Hi, I was calling to see if you have a youth choir."

"Well, not yet, we were trying to get a youth group going first."

"Do you have kids' programming?"

"Well, we have some kids, but they're not very programmed."

"OK; do you have a singles ministry?"

"Well, a lot of people are getting divorced around here, if that's what you mean."

"OK, goodbye."

It wasn't quite that bad, but sometimes it felt that way. Everybody wanted to be a part of a big church. We worked hard to grow and develop ministries for all kinds and types. Suddenly it happened. We grew and grew. Then a family who had been a part of our church for years came to me and said, "We feel God leading us to a smaller church." "What?" I said with panic in my voice. "This is just too big and we don't know anybody. We feel lost in all the activity." This was a real eye-opener for me. I came to the realization that bigger is not better and smaller is not better. Relationships are what make a church healthy.

> **❝ I came to the realization that bigger is not better and smaller is not better. Relationships are what make a church healthy. ❞**

Small-group relationships are a must if you want to impact people's lives in a meaningful way. The need for small groups is not going away. Our world is becoming more fragmented, disengaged, isolated, and immune to healthy relationships. People are searching for intimacy. Let's assume the responsibility for creating an environment of trust. If the church doesn't create this environment, who will?

An important thing to keep in mind as you begin small groups is that fellowship and community are central to the small-group experience. Don't be afraid that there isn't enough "solid teaching" going on in small groups. The more people talk with each other, the more they are building authentic community and connecting to the Body of Christ.

REPAIR 2: UNDERSTAND WHAT YOUR JOB IS.

As a pastor, I'm sometimes guilty of accepting responsibility for providing social connection for everyone. After all, isn't it our job to make certain that everybody is "feeling connected"?

My wife and I recently went to a social function in our community. I wasn't in charge and it had nothing to do with church.

I found myself walking around the room trying to make everyone feel connected. I walked from table to table greeting people. I was being my friendly self, shaking hands and assuming everyone would want to talk to me. My wife, Bonnie, looked at me kind of strangely and whispered, "What are you doing? This isn't church." I was attempting to keep everyone happy. I simply wanted to make sure they were all having a good time.

I felt really dumb when I realized what I was doing. I went back to my chair, sat down, and enjoyed the rest of the night without accepting the responsibility of keeping everyone connected. As people come into our churches, we tend to assume responsibility for their sense of connection. This is a big mistake. Our job is to provide opportunities for people to get involved.

I was speaking with a new family in our church a few weeks ago, and I asked them if they were getting involved. They told me that it was very difficult to get involved in our church. I asked them which service they attended. They said "It varies from week to week." I then asked them if they attended the midweek service. They informed me of their busy schedules. I asked if they had gotten into a small group. They told me that they had picked up some brochures, but they had not attended any of the groups. I learned from this experience and many others that people will often find a way to maintain their distance even when you offer all the right stuff.

REPAIR 3: SHOW TRUE EMOTION.

We've been thinking too religiously; we need to have some fun! Why is it that when people talk about the greatest parties they've ever attended, church socials don't come to mind? One of the most powerful ways to connect people is through laughter. We should have a great time enjoying the people of God.

Ask yourself these questions: "Do the people in my church laugh enough?" "Do they laugh at the right things?" One of the greatest tragedies in our culture today is that we allow Hollywood to define what we laugh at. Some of the sitcoms on television drive me crazy. Usually I find them sickening, not funny. Let's make a commitment to laugh more at the good stuff.

But fellowship is much more than laughter. It's the essence of Christ connecting to us through the power of his death and resurrection. It's the bond of God tying us together as his bride.

Do you cry enough? Do you cry enough for the right reasons? I'm not asking you to become a crybaby. But when is the last time you took to heart the pain and heartache of a brother or sister in Christ to the point that you wept? Jesus wept before he raised Lazarus from the dead. He also wept over the people of Jerusalem because they had no shepherd. It broke his heart.

Fellowship in God's family means sharing these extremes of emotion. Sometimes we need to take a few more risks and ask people to share more of their lives with us and with one another. We need to lead the way by sharing our hearts from the pulpit. We do this by being vulnerable, broken, caring, or humorous. Let's make a decision to have some fun in ministry. Clergypeople are often too serious. Enjoy the challenges and smell the roses. Be authentic and relational with your congregation. Stop standing off at a distance as an untouchable. Let 'em see ya sweat. Let 'em see ya bleed, and by all means, let 'em see ya' laugh.

> **66** Fellowship is much more than laughter. It's the essence of Christ connecting to us through the power of his death and resurrection. It's the bond of God tying us together as his bride. **99**

REPAIR 4: GET OUT—OF THE CHURCH WALLS, THAT IS.

Think *community*, not *church community*. It's interesting to see what happens when Christians venture beyond the walls of the church building. When Jesus called Matthew the tax collector to follow him, he stepped out of the ordinary religious circle. Matthew 9:9-12 says, "As Jesus went on from there, he saw a man named Matthew sitting at the tax collector's booth. 'Follow me,' he told him, and Matthew got up and followed him. While Jesus was having dinner at Matthew's house, many tax collectors and 'sinners' came and ate with him and his disciples. When the Pharisees saw this, they asked his disciples, 'Why does your teacher eat with tax collectors and "sinners"? On hearing this, Jesus said, 'It is not the healthy who need a doctor, but the sick.' "

Jesus modeled something for us here that's deeply challenging. We must be willing to connect with those outside the church walls. For too long we have asked people to break all ties with those "publicans and sinners," not realizing that God put those people in their lives for a reason. Of course we must be careful not to become like the world. But we must also be careful not to ignore the people in the world.

When we begin to train Christians to think *community* rather than *church community*, many changes will occur. They'll live out their Christianity with more impact and visibility. They'll not be able to compartmentalize their lives into church life, family life, work life, and social life. Instead, they'll be forced to be consistent in who they are in all the aspects of life. They'll realize the need to evangelize. Too many churchgoing people don't read the paper or know the names of their city leaders. After all, God is their source, and the church is their world. This is a real mistake. Christians need to interface with their culture to sense how needy it is.

Further, people will have opportunity for community leadership. God gives favor to Christians when they are willing to step out in faith and get involved in community events. I have watched many people in our church receive blessing from God because they have stepped out in community leadership. God does care about the poor. God does care about the earth; he created it, you know! God does care about widows and the needy. God does care about the fatherless. God does care about the children. As Christians, we need to accept the responsibility to be involved in many of the endeavors of our nation, our states, and our cities. We should be printing in our bulletins the wonderful opportunities to make a difference through civic involvement.

Best of all, people in your church will have the ability to make a difference in your community. As we encourage our churches to step out in community events, we'll be able to impact lives that we would never touch otherwise.

> 66 As we encourage our churches to step out in community events, we'll be able to impact lives that we would never touch otherwise. 99

Discipleship—Teaching People to Jump

REPAIR 1: BECOME AN EQUIPPING CHURCH.

What does it mean to equip someone? I remember a birthday card I received from my wife one year. It showed a picture of a little sky diver jumping out of a plane. On the inside, it said, "You are scheduled to jump out of a plane tomorrow." I had always wanted to go sky diving. I asked her if she had taken out a new life insurance policy on me (in jest, of course)!

I showed up at our local airport sky diving training center. I was about to go through a discipleship program I will never forget. Learning is what discipleship is all about, and I was eager to learn because I would be putting my life at risk. That has a way of getting your attention.

In church life, we need to create an atmosphere of lives at risk, because lives *are* at risk. If we believe that, it changes everything in regard to our eagerness to learn and disciple.

We started with the basics. The first thing we did was to learn about our equipment. They showed us the harness, the parachute, the clips, the spare 'chute, the rip cord, the boots, the helmet, and the goggles. I learned why I needed these things and how to use them effectively and properly. My life was at stake, so I was listening. I was learning the basics.

Many new Christians never really get basic training. They never learn about the critical equipment: the Bible, the concordance, the Bible dictionary, the devotional life, the prayer life, or the daily disciplines. Their lives are at stake, and yet we don't take the time to go through "boot camp" with them. Why should God allow the lost to find Christ in our church if we have no plan in place to train them for the life-risk they are taking? It's imperative that we get serious about teaching the basics to new Christians.

Our instructors walked us through a plethora of information. We learned that we would be jumping from about 3,500 feet above the ground. We learned that they would stall the airplane at a speed of about seventy miles an hour and that's when we would jump. We learned the importance of body position when leaving the airplane so we wouldn't get hung up on it. We learned to expect the jerk of the 'chute opening up. We learned what to do if our primary 'chute didn't open. We learned to keep our feet together and knees slightly bent to avoid breaking our legs on landing.

I fear that we don't thoroughly communicate to the Christian the importance of listening to God and reading his Word. The Word of God is the very thing that will keep us from so much of the pain in our lives. The safe way down (or should I say up?) is to live in his plan. Discipleship is the training that develops people into thinkers who can respond when the 'chute doesn't work, and land safely when the wind is threatening their marriages or their lives.

It was exciting to go into the room with the mock airplane. This was a model of a plane just like the plane we would be jumping from. We watched as our instructors went through the process of jumping out and reminded us of all we had learned. Then we climbed into position and went through the regimen: "Put your feet out, look up, jump." Over and over we said those words as we followed the command. They watched us and corrected us. They stood over us, viewing every detail of our positions as though our lives were at stake. I learned something that day: it mattered to our instructors that we made it. A lot *was* at stake. We continued practicing until the process, and commands of our instructors were comfortable and normal in our minds.

This entire process relates so well to the need to mentor new Christians. A lot is at stake in their lives. Our instructors were trained and focused. We must provide the same level of intensity for those getting ready to engage in a spiritual leap of faith.

I was nervous because I had never taken off in an airplane knowing that I wouldn't be landing in it. I was also excited. It was all happening so fast. "Put your feet out, look up, jump." I had heard the command a hundred times, but this time it was different. I was jumping from a much higher level. It was real.

Out I went. I'll always remember that moment of falling—hoping and believing that the 'chute on my back would do what it was supposed to do. I felt the abrupt jerk of my 'chute and looked up to examine the lines. All was well. I could now enjoy the ride.

> **66** When a person makes a faith commitment to Christ and becomes his disciple, there comes a moment when he or she must jump. **99**

What a picture! When a person makes a faith commitment to Christ and becomes his disciple, there comes a moment when he or she must jump. Jesus led his disciples to jump in this passage:

"As you go (jump), preach this message: 'The kingdom of heaven is near.' Heal the sick, raise the dead, cleanse those who have leprosy, drive out demons. Freely you have received, freely give. Do not take along any gold or silver or copper in your belts; take no bag for the journey, or extra tunic, or sandals or a staff; for the worker is worth his keep" (Matthew 10:7-10).

Jesus had provided the training, and it was time to jump. One of the shocking elements in my sky diving escapade is the fact that in one day, I went through the training and jumped from an airplane. I was not an expert, nor was I attempting any sky diving stunts. But I jumped. I really did it. Sometimes we forget that the new Christian needs to be released into ministry before he or she becomes an expert in theology. Jumping is the step that is often left out of our discipleship programs.

> **66** Sometimes we forget that the new Christian needs to be released into ministry before he or she becomes an expert in theology. Jumping is the step that is often left out of our discipleship programs. **99**

The thrill for me was the jump. The thrill for the new Christian is the jump. It's that moment when the Holy Spirit prompts the sharing of faith for the very first time. It's that moment of being at the mercy of God to bring the answer to the question just asked. It's that moment of trusting God with the first tithe check. It's that moment of being asked to teach or share a Bible study. These are the moments when Christians experience the thrill of the jump. These are the times when they feel the thrill of walking in obedience to our God.

Ask people to share their story. Ask them to lead in prayer. Ask them to jump and they'll jump. We have far too many trained jumpers in the pew that have never taken their first jump. They're bored, tired, and cynical. To wake them up we need to put 'chutes on their backs and push them out of the plane. They'll stop whining and start flying.

I experienced a few wonderful moments floating through the air that day. I looked around, enjoying the beautiful Colorado mountains. I could see so much, and I felt every moment.

I looked down and noticed that the ground was coming toward me very quickly. It felt as though I wasn't moving but that the earth was racing toward me. I remembered what my instructor had asked me as we took off.

"Dary, how much did you say you weigh?"

"210," I replied.

"How tall are you?" she asked.

"6'4," I replied.

She got this funny look on her face, and I asked, "What?"

She then said, "The 'chute you have on is a large, but you really need an extra large. The one you have on is for someone who weighs about 185 pounds. But don't worry, I've watched you; you're athletic, you'll be fine. Just keep those legs together."

Suddenly, as I was floating through the air, the landing part didn't seem so fun. I decided to stop the journey right there. "I don't want to land. Come and get me right here. I quit." Wrong! It was a little late for that.

We often prepare new Christians for the flight by telling them about forgiveness, peace, love, joy, and contentment. Then, once they're flying, we tell them about the landing. We might want to warn people about the landing before the jump. We need to tell people that it's a challenge to live in holiness before our God. We need to prepare people for the depth of the commitment it takes to honor God. If we don't tell them, they could break their legs and never jump again. Thankfully, I survived the landing, even though I did hurt one of my knees a bit.

I have this first jump on videotape, and I can see that I didn't keep my legs together upon impact. I opened them up out of habit from other mountain sports. The point is this: we learn lessons best by experience rather than by hearing about them in the classroom. It may be painful, but it's more effective. I challenge you to find ways to disciple people and release them into a meaningful ministry. Have fun!

REPAIR 2: SHARE THE RESPONSIBILITY OF MINISTRY.

It's interesting to watch churches take the risk of releasing people into meaningful ministry. All across our nation, we're seeing a new breed of churches that believe in their people. "Recruit, train, and release" has become the new pattern of church culture. The result has been that we're seeing healthier churches. As people get involved in the work of the ministry, they care more, give more, attend more, and pray more. Wow, what a concept! When you talk to people who are involved in ministry, they're excited and challenged by the thrill of the jump and sobered by the responsibility. I like that.

Volunteers help us solve some of the greatest challenges we face as a church. As pastors, we often pride ourselves on being the men or women of God who have been sent to speak the answers. The truth is, we rarely have the answers. God has a way of bringing solutions through means other than us.

Do you trust others? Will you share your responsibilities with others—the vision, the pulpit, the hat of authority? There are many things we're willing to give up, but a few we aren't. I believe opening the garage door to the new Christian means we're willing to share more of our role than ever before.

The church world has become accustomed to the pastor in the leadership role. People are content to let the limitations of the leader limit the vision. After all, "What more can he do?" they think. These days, in the business world, corporations and growing companies are sharing vision and power more than ever. There are more mergers of big companies than ever before in our history. It's because these companies have learned that they can do more together than they can do apart.

> **❝** A church limits its potential when its leader tries to assume all ministry responsibility. A gifted pastor can lead large numbers of people with this philosophy, but eventually, the church will reach a place of stagnation. **❞**

Companies are shifting to leadership teams rather than having leaders make the decisions on their own. A church limits its potential when the leader tries to assume all ministry responsibility. A gifted pastor can lead large numbers of people with this philosophy, but eventually, the church will reach a place of stagnation.

Let's talk about how to release ministry. You need to develop an eye for leaders. Create a list of the names of people in whom you see leadership qualities. Meet with them individually or call a meeting with that group to help you lead your church. Here are some tips to help you develop leaders:

Release authority and responsibility slowly; there's no hurry. A mistake in this area can be costly. Take your time, but do it. Also be sure to release authority and responsibility together. There's nothing worse than having responsibility and no authority. Make it a point to empower people to do all that they are held accountable for.

Clearly articulate the vision with these leaders. Make certain they understand your heart and your vision. Establish clear lines of communication. Make certain your leaders have access to you during the first stages of taking over the reins of leadership; someone may have a one-minute question that saves a three-week brawl.

Correct mistakes quickly. I've gone to leaders in our church many times to ask why they made certain decisions. After listening carefully to their reasoning, I owe it to them to share whether I believe a decision to be a wrong one. Sometimes you can't undo someone's decision, and you must stand by him or her through the process. However, it will help that person in the future if you spend the time sharing your thought processes with him or her. I'm not suggesting that you judge every decision that everyone makes. That would be absurd. I'm saying that if someone makes a decision that's wrong, they need to hear the details of your thought process about it—not in anger, but in love. This will improve their ability to make big decisions in the future.

Be willing to admit you're wrong. This will save you a lot of grief. When you become a healthy role model for your team to follow, they'll be healthy leaders that you can trust. When you say, "I blew it," it can be like a salve to the wound of a leader who has recently blown it. Let's face it—if you don't blow it once in a while, you're not leading aggressively enough. When you live under the paranoia of making an error, you'll lock up and fail to lead anything.

> 66 Let's face it—if you don't blow it once in a while, you're not leading aggressively enough. When you live under the paranoia of making an error, you'll lock up and fail to lead anything. 99

Give healthy evaluations. Good feedback and constructive criticism can keep people connected to you and to God. I work under the premise that I can always do something better than I am doing it right now. I'm not picky about who corrects me, because I want to improve and exalt God in my life.

Match tasks with abilities. Keep doing the task until you can find a gifted person who can learn to do the task well. Someone will eventually do it as well as you, better than you, and definitely differently than you. Let it happen!

REPAIR 3: MEASURE SUCCESS WITHOUT STRESS.

How can we measure the success of a church or a leader? When is a hospital visit successful? When is a sermon successful? How do you know when a staff meeting has been effective? These kinds of questions can drive a church leader crazy.

Let me offer a simple list you can use to measure success without spending hours fretting over it. Measure success through the following filters:

- Do the followers view the correct person as the leader?
- Are goals and objectives being set and accomplished?
- Is turnover within leadership teams of the ministry minimal?
- Is the ministry free from a constant flow of patterned criticism?
- Is there healthy energy and excitement coming from the ministry?

REPAIR 4: HOLD VOLUNTEERS ACCOUNTABLE.

Sometimes we've been afraid to hold volunteers accountable. After all, they're not getting paid to do their jobs. It's a difficult and touchy subject. How can you expect accountability from a volunteer? Although volunteerism is an old concept in the church, it works and will continue to be a wonderful way to involve people.

You can hold volunteers accountable in a number of ways. Here are a few:

• Establish a job description for each job and then have the proper person review it each year with the volunteer.

• Have quarterly meetings for volunteers, and have each person give an update on his or her area of ministry. If you're in a large church, maybe each ministry area could hold its own volunteer meeting.

• Help each volunteer establish yearly goals for his or her area of ministry. This will help them avoid falling into routine and maintenance.

• Build in some kind of accountability through "touch bases" and open communication. When volunteers work for long periods of time without reporting or communicating what's happening, poor performance often occurs.

Evangelism: Reaching Hurting People

REPAIR 1: EMPHASIZE RELATIONAL EVANGELISM.

For many years, the goal of the church has been to evangelize the world. Makes sense! Jesus said to "Go into all the world and preach the good news." Without a doubt, we should obey this command. However, one of the challenges we face in our postmodern world is that mass evangelism is less effective than in the past. America has changed. People aren't lining up to become Christians as they did in the Billy Graham era. Our methods of reaching people for Christ need repair. Let's put them on the bench and take a look at them.

When we open the garage door to bring people to Christ today, things look radically different from the evangelism models of the past. Impersonal, guilt-ridden sermons push people away from Christ. Postmoderns are skeptical and judgmental of Christians whose primary goal is to convert them. They don't like being targeted like fish in a nearby lake just waiting to bite the hook. They resent us for treating them all the same. They've become aware of our evangelism tactics, training classes, and one-hour outreaches.

> **66** People without Christ smell our old fish nets. They're not interested in the four spiritual laws and they don't care about our personal experiences unless they know us first. **99**

People are weary of our attempts to lure them into our net without caring for them as people first—I mean really caring for them. We often say things like, "We love their souls" or "We care about where they spend eternity." These are fine statements, but they aren't complete enough. Reaching people today takes greater commitment than we have ever known. People without Christ smell our old fish nets. They're not interested in the four spiritual laws and they don't care about our personal experiences unless they know us first. The only reason they might "pray a prayer with us" is to get rid of us.

They sense that it's our need, not theirs, that drives us. It's our need to brag about the fish we caught. Or it's our need to tell the story to other fishermen along the bank who had little success. Or it's our need to measure and weigh the catch to determine our value. They know it's about us, and we desperately need to put it on the workbench to fix it.

REPAIR 2: VALUE ALL PEOPLE.

I am amazed at the way people who don't know Christ have been devalued in the name of God. Jesus was so sensitive to this issue that he told a story about it. In Luke 10:31, he told about a church leader's reaction to a man who was beaten up, robbed, and left to die beside the road: "A priest happened to be going down the same road, and when he saw the man, he passed by on the other side."

66 We've grown so accustomed to leading our followers that we've passed by the masses of people who've been ripped off by a culture that has stripped and beaten them into despair. 99

This is a frightening picture of what has happened to many of us. We've grown so accustomed to leading our followers that we've passed by the masses of people who've been ripped off by a culture that has stripped and beaten them into despair. We don't really see them. We're caught up in church. We're focused on buildings, ministries, leadership seminars, staff, and projects.

Most of us don't think this passage applies to us. It does! This is the story Jesus told to get the attention of the clergy of his day. Please put yourself in this story. Don't let it slip by. Think about how relevant this is to your everyday life. We're on the very same road where the wounded, beaten, and broken are lying. They need us. They need our strength and encouragement. They need our care and concern. They need our tears. They need our broken hearts. They need our time and compassion. They need us to look at them, to see them, and to feel what they feel. They need us to stop hurrying by them—to stop doing church and determine to be the church.

We've lost our understanding of what it means to value one person. Do we leave the ninety-nine to go after the one? We want to grow our church. We want to experience all that God has for us. We want to tell the world. But stop right now and let God reveal to you the times you've passed them by: the grocery-store clerk, the bank teller, the neighbor whose dog is driving you crazy, and the kids you despise because of their pierced parts and tattoos. These are the broken masses. These are the ones we devalue when we pass them by. Luke 10:32-35 says,

"So too, a Levite, when he came to the place and saw him, passed by on the other side. But a Samaritan, as he traveled, came where the man was; and when he saw him, he took pity on him. He went to him and bandaged his wounds, pouring on oil and wine. Then he put the man on his own donkey, took him to an inn and took care of him. The next day he took out two silver coins and gave them to the innkeeper. 'Look after him,' he said, 'and when I return, I will reimburse you for any extra expense you may have.' "

The Samaritan "came to where the man was." We, too, must leave the path of clergy comfort. We must shock people by where we go and who we care for. We need to leave the schedule and pressure and walk down a path less traveled to find the hurting ones. We must go to where they are.

This Samaritan actually "saw" the beaten man. He didn't see him as a member, a helper, a giver, a partner, or a teammate. He just saw him as he was—lying there, beaten, broken, wounded, robbed, and devalued. May God put a spiritual twenty-twenty vision in the eyes of the pastors of America. We need to see with the eyes of God.

The Samaritan also "took pity on him." Pity comes as a result of caring. Do you see the natural order in this text: going, seeing, and caring? This is the essence of valuing mankind. The Samaritan got involved in the process of healing. Let's get involved in the process of caring and valuing people in such a way that we can feel the favor and blessing of God shining through us again.

Valuing people who don't know Christ means we spend time with them. It means spending energy exchanging true friendship. It means spending money doing, going, and being with them. We're not primarily interested in the catch but rather in the fulfillment of finding friendships. We believe in them because God created them and values them. When Jesus said he would make his disciples "fishers of men," he didn't intend for them to treat people with the same value as they treat fish. We often miss seeing the need for relationships with people. When we put evangelism on the workbench, we see it in its broken state.

REPAIR 3: HELP NEW CHRISTIANS ADJUST.

I was so tickled at a recent wedding that I almost burst out laughing right in the middle of the ceremony. One of the flower girls was standing in front on the platform looking carefully at all of the guests. Suddenly her eyes lit up and she put her hands between her legs and shouted out, "I have to go potty right now." The whole place roared with laughter. People were momentarily paralyzed. No one moved. She shouted again, "Somebody better come and help me." Finally, a family member went to her aid, and out the side door they went. Close call. This story is one of many we could all share of funny things that happen in church. The little girl didn't know the rules of church or of weddings. She was responding the best way she knew how to the trial she was facing.

When people find Jesus for the first time, they're completely in the dark about church expectations. They don't understand church culture. They are often dealing with issues that we've been afraid to talk about from the pulpit. They feel the need to ask questions and experience this new way of living. I have asked new Christians to share with me the things that confuse them about church. These are a few of the things that made them apprehensive:

- unwritten dress codes
- lack of ashtrays
- standing
- singing
- where they fit
- getting involved

We need to do our best to help new Christians adjust to their experience at church.

REPAIR 4: TRAIN CHRISTIANS TO SHARE THEIR LIVES.

I am saddened by the separation of life and faith. Many evangelism methods are more about the *steps* we walk people through rather than the *lives* we live. Have you ever stopped to ponder if we have made it more difficult than it really is? Maybe sharing our faith with others is as easy as sharing our lives with them. Perhaps the reason it's so difficult for us to share our lives with others is because our lives aren't authentic. We have fallen into the church subculture and have learned how to smile and say "Praise God" in the right place at the right time.

Let's train people to believe that evangelism and reaching others is simply sharing our lives in truth and

66 Perhaps the reason it's so difficult for us to share our lives with others is because our lives aren't authentic. 99

honesty. It's about sharing our hurts, needs, time, and energy with others who will feel free to do the same. Opening the garage door and exposing the truth about who we are will be refreshing to the person who has pasted the Darwin sticker on his trunk. A relational-evangelism training class may look something like this:

- Class One: Live life to the fullest
- Class Two: Live life to the fullest in front of others
- Class Three: Talk to other people in your world
- Class Four: Talk about others more than you talk about yourself
- Class Five: Build a bridge to people through genuine love and care
- Class Six: Be available when people have a crisis or trust you enough to ask for your help
- Class Seven: Tell people about the power and hope of your life: Jesus Christ
- Class Eight: Bring someone else through these classes

This is probably a very simplistic view of garage-door evangelism, but it works.

Let's help people understand that their lives are their greatest witness.

REPAIR 5: ASSIMILATE NEW CHRISTIANS INTO CHURCH LIFE.

I'm frustrated to say that in most cases, when a new Christian joins a typical church, he or she becomes spiritually crippled within six months. I'm not trying to be hurtful; I'm humbled by the fact that this has happened too often in the church I pastor. It's difficult for new Christians to truly enter into the lifeblood of the local church. We're working on it.

I believe this problem exists because of three primary factors:

- We are not ready to respond to new Christians.
- We don't have enough ministry opportunities for new Christians.

> **❝ In most cases, when a new Christian joins a typical church, he or she becomes spiritually crippled within six months. ❞**

• We have few mature Christians who will give time to new Christians.

New Christians will not assimilate naturally. It takes forethought, planning, and commitment to make the transition successful. Assimilation could save new Christians from years of heartache and spiritual crippling. Isn't it worth it?

Ministry: Releasing People to Serve

REPAIR 1: REDEFINE MINISTRY.

If you were to ask the typical churchgoing person if he or she is a minister, he or she would look at you like you had lost your mind. The biblical word "minister" simply means "one who serves" or "servant." If you were to ask a typical churchgoing person if he or she serves in a ministry, the question would make more sense to that person.

We have typically defined ministry as something that requires hours and hours of training and equipping before people can serve. The new Christian needs to come to a quick understanding that ministry is simply serving God in a meaningful way.

As a church leader, I have learned most of my lessons the hard way. I am still learning every day, and I have a long way to go. One lesson I learned the hard way is that our ministry must reach outside our church walls. Before we realized it, all the ministries our church offered were happening within our walls and were being led by people inside our church. We had devalued critical ministries such as parenting, serving as leaders in the community through volunteering for certain leadership boards, volunteering in public or Christian schools, and giving time to help soccer clubs or other sports clubs that influence young people. We tend to view these kinds of activities as extras rather than actual ministries. We have made a mistake by placing a higher value on ushering at church than on volunteering in the school one's child attends.

We asked people to look at their lives and list the places they have influence every day, every week, and every month of the year. It shocked them to discover that God has already given them opportunities for ministry. They had simply never recognized them as such. Most of these ministry opportunities don't fit in the "profiles" we have put together for people to look through.

Teaching people that ministry is a lifestyle rather than an event can require patience and repetition. Ask yourself this question: How can we get people to view their everyday involvement in things as a ministry unto God? This can be as simple as a mom who picks up her child every day from school offering to bring her neighbor's child home to save them a trip to town. This is a ministry. We must start defining this as a ministry and allowing people to view their lives as "ministry saturated." The people in our churches aren't effective in everyday ministries because we have never placed value on them. Once they begin to understand the value God places on the everyday routine, our congregations will become more sensitive to allowing daily routines to be filled with "God moments."

When I was a youth pastor in Denver, a young man in our community became a Christian. He was a professional motorcycle-racer but he was thinking of quitting. Then we began to talk about the guys he raced with. They were needy and had many issues they needed to deal with. Through the course of a few months, he developed a way to share his testimony with them. They began to respond—some positively, some negatively. This young man began to view his everyday world as a ministry that God had called him to and given him the talent for. What a concept!

> **❝** We must help people discover that ministry is not only signing up to be on the cleanup team after the meal. It's an opportunity to serve outside the church in the ways God has equipped them to serve. **❞**

We must help people discover that ministry is not only signing up to be on the cleanup team after the meal. It's an opportunity to serve outside the church in the ways God has equipped them to serve. We do this by placing a higher value on the outside-the-walls ministries. Share the concept of everyday evangelism in your sermons and have people share the "God moments" they've experienced within their outside-the-walls ministries. This will have a profound effect on those sitting in the pews who have not signed up for anything lately.

REPAIR 2: RECRUIT MINISTERS EFFECTIVELY

"Good morning, church. We welcome you here this morning on the day that the Lord has made. We will rejoice and be glad in it. Before we get started today, we need to ask a couple of you to help us in the nursery. Would you please help us?" Long pause. "Pleeeeeeease?" Sister So-and-So stands up and makes her way to the nursery.

That story inspires you to be a part of such a thriving ministry, doesn't it? This may be an exaggeration, but the point is clear. Here are a few suggestions to make recruitment a little more effective:

• Create a good job description.

• Establish an understanding of the schedule and the hours required.

• Develop a profile of the ministry gifts or personal strengths necessary.

• Make clear the duration of the need. Is this ministry permanent or temporary?

• Provide an opportunity for people to ask questions before signing on.

• Schedule an interview to go through the details of the ministry.

• Ask for a decision to get involved.

• Inform people abundantly. People who don't sign on are often just saying, "Tell me more." The more information we can give, the better chance we have of someone catching that vision.

Only occasionally do we ask for volunteers through our bulletin. These are usually ministries like helping take down the set after a production or serving as ushers at a big event. We have learned that the best recruiting takes place through one-on-one relationships. Ask current workers to submit names of people they know who might have an interest in the ministry, and then follow up in person.

By placing the five priorities of the church on the workbench, you are hopefully committing to opening your garage door. Fixing each of the areas may not always be easy or quick, but you can be sure it will be worth it!

Garage-Door Openers

1. List two or three items in your church that need to be placed on the workbench and examined.

2. What can you do personally to worship God in spirit and in truth more fully?

3. How would small groups improve your ministry?

4. What would happen in your church if everyone began to think *community* rather than *church community*?

5. List ways that you could release people into meaningful ministry.

6. How does your church show that it values people? How does it show that it devalues people?

7. What new ministries need to be developed in the church you lead?

Chapter 4

The Electrical Box:

THE PROPER RELEASE OF POWER

Most homes across America don't have built-in generators. They depend on an outside energy source. This is a beautiful picture of our dependence on the Holy Spirit. We have no power to build the church except the power that comes from the Holy Spirit. This doesn't deny or minimize the leadership gifts God has given us. It simply reminds us that we cannot do our job without a true dependence upon God.

We must focus our efforts on tapping into God's power rather than on attempting to create power. When pastors try to create power, a couple of things happen: First, they're tempted to try to force the light to come on even when the power is out. If you've ever experienced a power outage in your home, you understand this thought. You flip the switch again and again until it sinks in that the light switch has very little to do with the power. The light switch releases the power, but it doesn't create it; it's not the source.

When the lights aren't coming on in your ministry, don't stand and flip the switch on and off, over and over. If you're reacting to breakdown in your ministry in this way, you're probably extremely frustrated and disappointed. What you must realize is that there's no light because the power isn't flowing. Until you find out why the power is cut off, you'll continue in your frustration and eventually lose hope.

> 66 Until you find out why the power is cut off, you'll continue in your frustration and eventually lose hope. 99

The Battle for Power

There is a constant battle for power in our lives. The world, our flesh, and the forces of evil try to pull us away from God's power. This spiritual war is usually fought in silence, but it's real. I'm not trying to be spooky, but there have been times in my life when Satan has battled against my mind and my emotions, trying to create depression, discouragement, and doubt. Many pastors are fighting the same battle, and they're losing. Church leaders are becoming more weary and tired than ever before. Their power is being drained by a silent war.

When Bonnie and I lived in Grand Junction, Colorado, we were awakened one night by a very loud noise. It came from the bathroom just down the hall from our bedroom. Bonnie asked, "Did you hear that?" I whispered back, "Yes." With all the courage and strength I could muster, I said, "I'll pray while you go check it out." She didn't go for that.

I got out of bed and grabbed a stick from the corner of our room. I slowly and quietly made my way around our bed to the door of our bedroom. The door was cracked open, and I peeked through, like a detective peering into an abandoned building. There was nothing in the hall.

I prayed and walked into the bathroom. I quickly turned on the light—there was no one there. However, the shower curtain was closed. I felt like I was in a scene from a horror movie.

My heart was pounding; the adrenaline was flowing in my veins. I braced myself, pulled back the shower curtain, and saw that the nylon netting that held the toys for our children's baths had fallen off the wall and landed in the bathtub. It was a fish net holder that contained boats, rubber duckies, and other toys for our children. The suction cup that was designed to hold the net against the tile wall had come loose.

This incident illustrates a silent war. There was a continual battle going on between gravity and that suction cup to retain its grip and position on the wall. No one could hear or see the battle, but there was a constant struggle. When gravity finally won the battle, the net and all the toys crashed into the tub.

> 66 The enemy of your soul is pushing down on you, just as the weight of a vehicle pushes down on its tires. If you lose the battle, you'll never tap into the true source of power. 99

An automobile also illustrates a silent war. There is constant tension and pressure inside car tires. They're in a never-ending battle to hold up the weight of the car. Between the rim and the tire, there is tremendous air pressure. The struggle going on between the air pressure holding up the car and the car pushing down is like the pull of the enemy against your soul, spirit, and mind.

The enemy of your soul is pushing down on you, just as the weight of a vehicle pushes down on its tires. If you lose the battle, you'll never tap into the true source of power. You'll never have the faith to believe God for the simple things that he has promised unless you win this silent battle.

The Leading of the Spirit

Because the Holy Spirit is the source of our power, being led by the Spirit is essential. However, being led by the Spirit means different things to different people. There are people in the church who have taken this phrase to dangerous extremes. They believe that being led by the Spirit means to abandon wisdom and knowledge, releasing the steering wheel of the car to go wherever it may go. This is certainly not my idea of being led by the Spirit.

> 66 Being led by the Spirit means connecting your heart, mind, and soul to the Spirit of the living God. 99

Being led by the Spirit means connecting your heart, mind, and soul to the Spirit of the living God. It's your nature being connected to the nature of God. It's your thoughts being birthed by the Spirit of God, your actions being developed by the Spirit of God, and your disciplines being cultivated by the Spirit of God.

Matthew 4:1 says, "Then Jesus was led by the Spirit into the desert to be tempted by the devil." The word "led" used in this verse literally means to depart, to loose, to set forth, and (my favorite of all) to launch or to sail away. The word "spirit" here is "pneuma." As we saw in Chapter 3, "pneuma" is a current of air, a breath, or a breeze.

> 66 When you are filled to capacity with the breath or wind of God, when you hear the voice of God, and when you respond in obedience to God, that's when the power of God is manifested in your life. 99

Combining the words "led" and "spirit" creates a powerful word picture. "Led by the Spirit" can literally mean "sail away with the breath or wind of God." This is critical as it relates to power. God creates the wind, and only God can fill the sail with his breath (his Spirit). The ship moves only as its sail is filled with wind. Wind is not something we can create or generate. It's a God thing. Aren't you glad? I certainly am.

As we lead churches, how many times do we wait for the wind to fill our sails? How many times do we try to create the wind ourselves? When you are filled to capacity with the breath or wind of God, when you hear the voice of God, and when you respond in obedience to God, that's when the power of God is manifested in your life. The church is empowered when its leadership is empowered by God. The wind fills the sail, and the Holy Spirit takes us to the right destination.

When Bonnie and I built our house north of Fort Collins, we watched the installation of all the electrical wiring, outlets, and switches. There were rolls of wire pulled into various parts of the house. The wire had to make its way into every room. The electricians finished their work and flipped the switch. The house was empowered! It was a wonderful moment!

This is a beautiful picture of what happens when a church trusts God to be the source of power. We build buildings and create structures and then God empowers them. He creates the energy and power to impact a community. He empowers his church to fulfill his great and perfect plan.

Breakers, Light Switches, Light Bulbs, and Outlets

After God empowers the house, there are several important elements to consider about the use of his power.

BREAKERS

> **It's a major problem when the senior pastor believes he or she is the only breaker for every department, issue, and decision.**

Breakers are built to monitor and distribute power. They don't blow up. They don't get frustrated. They don't get jealous. They stack one on top of the other with the assurance that the power will flow through them to the proper places. If you open the electrical panel-box in the garage or wherever it may be in your home, you'll probably find a list of rooms that coincide with the numbers next to the breakers. This is so you'll know which breaker controls which area of the house.

Apply the imagery of breakers to the healthy release of power in the church you lead. Ministry leaders need to be empowered to make decisions concerning the issues related to their ministries. It's a major problem when the senior pastor believes he or she is the only breaker for every department, issue, and decision. This overloads the breaker, causing it to pop. The breaker switch can no longer support the use of power that's trying to flow through it.

I've watched pastors break. They can no longer handle the stress of making every decision in the church, and yet they try to hold on and cling to the power they feel is theirs to control. This is not God's design. God wants you to release power in the church in a healthy fashion, just as a breaker box does in a house.

There are many breakers in the box. You can't do it all. That's God's job. It's your job to distribute the power to the leaders of each segment of your church. Power and the use of power will make you or break you as a pastor.

Take a moment to think through the release of power in your church. Ask God to reveal the power areas you need to release. The only way to release power throughout the house is to trust the breaker. You must trust the leader, the staff pastor, and others to whom you are giving authority. You must cultivate strong relationships so that when the power comes through the box, you can be confident it will reach the room.

> 66 The only way to release power throughout the house is to trust the breaker. You must trust the leader, the staff pastor, and others to whom you are giving authority. 99

Once the power is flowing properly into the rooms of the house, you'll be able to enjoy the benefits. Remember the words of 1 Corinthians 12:12-27?

"The body is a unit, though it is made up of many parts; and though all its parts are many, they form one body. So it is with Christ. For we were all baptized by one Spirit into one body—whether Jews or Greeks, slave or free—and we were all given the one Spirit to drink. Now the body is not made up of one part but of many. If the foot should say, 'Because I am not a hand, I do not belong to the body,' it would not for that reason cease to be part of the body. And if the ear should say, 'Because I am not an eye, I do not belong to the body,' it would not for that reason cease to be part of the body. If the whole body were an eye, where would the sense of hearing be? If the whole body were an ear, where would the sense of smell be? But in fact God has arranged the parts in the body, every one of them, just as he wanted them to be. If they were all one part, where would the body be? As it is, there are many parts, but one body. The eye cannot say to the hand, 'I don't need you!' And the head cannot say to the feet, 'I don't need you!' On the contrary, those parts of the body that seem to be weaker are indispensable, and the parts that we think are less honorable we treat with special honor. And the parts that are unpresentable are treated with special modesty, while our presentable parts need no special treatment. But God has combined the members of the body and has given greater honor to the parts that lacked it, so that there should be no division in the body, but that its parts should have equal concern for each other. If one part suffers, every part suffers with it; if one part is honored, every part rejoices with it. Now you are the body of Christ, and each one of you is a part of it."

This passage is a picture of a church empowered by God. Each one is doing his or her part as God empowers him or her. Imagine how different your church could be if everyone was empowered for service!

LIGHT SWITCHES

Most of us walk into a room and turn on the light without thinking about the process that occurs. We usually don't think about the fact that there's a great source of power somewhere miles away that's generating the energy coming into the electrical box. It flows through the mains to the breaker boxes and then to the wires that carry it to the room where there's a switch that can be turned on to tap into the power. We don't need to fully understand how it all works in order to flip on a switch. We simply trust the switch to release the power to the light bulb, and we have light.

There are times in the life of the house or the church when a switch goes bad. When a switch no longer releases the power to the bulb, it doesn't mean that the entire breaker or the breaker box needs to be replaced. Maybe the switch just needs to be replaced.

There may be times in your ministry when the light is supposed to come on, but it doesn't—the switch is bad. The power is flowing, but it can't be tapped into. This happened at Timberline Church. There are several people in our church who help prepare and serve dinners after a funeral in our fellowship. These people are faithful, and they do a great job. During my meeting with the family of the deceased, I had communicated that we would be happy to provide a meal. There was only one problem: I forgot to relay this information to the people in charge of providing meals. The day before the funeral, my secretary asked me if we were providing a meal for this family (thank God for a good secretary!). I said, "Yes," and then it dawned on me that I had not made proper arrangements.

> 66 There may be times in your ministry when the light is supposed to come on, but it doesn't—the switch is bad. The power is flowing, but it can't be tapped into. 99

This is an example of a bad switch. The power box worked fine, we had the people in place, and all the necessary wiring was intact to bring the power to the room and turn on the light. But the switch didn't work, so the light couldn't come on. The switch in this case was communication. Communication is the greatest tool of effective power-management in the church. It takes a tremendous amount of communication to keep the power source flowing to the right places.

If you've ever watched an electrician wire a house, you know that all the electricity flowing through that house has a place of connection; that's what makes it work. This is also true in church life. Our ministry leaders must have solid communication connections to be able to turn on the lights. Make certain that the flowchart of communication is clear and effective, or you'll be without light in the room.

> 66 In church life, people get burned out quickly, and we need to refresh and encourage them so that the light can continue to shine in the church and in the community. 99

LIGHT BULBS

At times the switch is fine, but the light bulb is burned out and needs to be replaced. In church life, people get burned out quickly, and we need to refresh and encourage them so that the light can continue to shine in the church and in the community. A healthy switch with a bad light bulb equals no light, but it doesn't mean the switch needs to be replaced. Again, deal with the right issues and make sure you understand the flow of power through the system.

OUTLETS

Think of an outlet in a room as an invitation. When you walk into the room and see an outlet, you realize immediately that behind that outlet is the power of the house, inviting you to tap into it. People entering the house can choose to tap into the power or ignore it, but it's there for their convenience and use.

Churches need a lot of outlets. These are invitations to people who walk into the garage. When people look around, they need to see an ample supply of power. There's nothing more frustrating than being in a house and needing to tap into power and finding no outlet or an outlet that doesn't work.

One of our goals as a church is to provide as many useable outlets as we possibly can in each room of our ministry. These outlets are invitations to people who want to test the power of God. Many times these outlets are needed for short-term use, like praying for people after a service. Ministries such as twelve-step ministries, recovery groups, small groups, marriage ministries, divorce-recovery groups, and rehabilitation groups all need to have outlets visible to the hurting people sitting in the pews. When these people hear about and see the outlets, they might be willing to plug in. And once they plug in, we hope and pray they'll be exposed to the power of Almighty God through the working of the Holy Spirit in that room.

One caution we need to understand is that electrical power can kill. There are too many stories about someone who became foolish or careless or was simply ignorant about power. We must keep in mind that the power of God is a very serious thing. The release of that power is also very serious.

> 66 Trying to embrace and release power without being grounded to the Word of God through the Holy Spirit will absolutely destroy you and everyone you touch. 99

In order for electrical power to be safely utilized in a house it must be grounded. When the electrician connects the power to the electrical box, he or she must make certain that it's properly grounded. Trying to embrace and release power without being grounded in the Word of God through the Holy Spirit will absolutely destroy you and everyone you touch. Are you grounded? Are you tapped into the source? Are you releasing what you have been given?

Garage-Door Openers

1. How is God reminding you that he's the source of your power?

2. In what ways is the Spirit of God leading you? Where do you believe he is taking you?

3. How is power released in your church. Is it a healthy release of power? Why or why not?

4. What plug-in points do newcomers see in your church? How can you make your outlets more visible and inviting?

5. What are some weaknesses in your ministry concerning power that you need to overcome?

6. List the ways that you are staying grounded.

Chapter 5

The Attic:

THE PRIVATE WORLD

I n my garage, there's a door in the ceiling with a rope hanging down. Beyond the door lies some really spooky stuff. I've been gathering items up in that attic for years. It's the place where darkness prevails and the heat of summer invades. Very few people ever go into the attic of my home. It's a place reserved for the strong and the brave. I only go there if I know the item I need is there. It's not a place for recreation. It's neither heated nor cooled. It's raw, and it's real. I have items in the attic from the past that I'll probably never use again, and I have items that are projects for the future. They're waiting for me to get them done.

All churches have spiritual "attics." The attic of the church is the place of both past and future. It often contains the history of strife, bad decisions, mistrust, and brokenness. It also contains the many past discussions about the future—the ideas, dreams, and vision that were once on the table during important meetings. These dreams were "tabled." They were placed in the attic for who knows how long.

Many times during the past twenty years of ministry, I've had a precious elderly person tell me a story that began with the words, "Well, Pastor, I remember back in the '50s…" Whatever era they pick, I realize that I'm about to hear an attic story. Attic stories are complicated because they always have personal memories and emotions wrapped up with them. Attic stories are real, challenging, and important. The importance of an attic story is not so much the story itself, but the revelation of the heart of the person telling the story. These attic stories are the best recollections people have about church history. Many memories about an incident or issue may be based entirely on opinion or misinformation; people have come to conclusions about matters that may not have ever had conclusions.

The things that linger in the attic are there for a reason. They either were never finished or they were finished in such a way that they didn't have proper closure. A visit to the church attic requires caution and careful understanding of the risks. You may think those issues are dead issues. You may assume no one really cares

> **"** The pastor of an established church who doesn't take the attic issues seriously will fail to lead the church into any meaningful change. **"**

any more about those decisions. But you're wrong. People are strange in this way. They keep their feelings attached to the emotions of the past. When those emotions are touched, all the attached feelings come screaming to the surface. This is why it's very difficult to help lead a church through change. It's much more pleasant to plant a new church and start fresh because there's not yet an established attic. If you are pastoring an established church and trying to lead it through change, you will need to understand the attic issues. The pastor of an established church who doesn't take the attic issues seriously will fail to lead the church into any meaningful change.

The nature of attic issues shifts with time. Some issues remain "hot button," personal issues while other issues grow cold as people get apathetic toward them over time. It becomes the pastor's role to help clean out the attic. This passage in Exodus will help you understand:

"The whole Israelite community set out from Elim and came to the Desert of Sin, which is between Elim and Sinai, on the fifteenth day of the second month after they had come out of Egypt. In the desert the whole community grumbled against Moses and Aaron. The Israelites said to them, 'If only we had died by the Lord's hand in Egypt! There we sat around pots of meat and ate all the food we wanted, but you have brought us out into this desert to starve this entire assembly to death' " (Exodus 16:1-3).

The Israelites were very excited to cross the Red Sea and partner with Moses and God. They had vision. They were willing and ready to take some risks. They also had seen the most incredible miracles ever performed. These miracles helped calm their doubts and fears. These experiences became part of their history, their heritage, their memory, and their attic. But as soon as the Israelites were weary, hungry, thirsty, and needy, they wandered back in time to the comfort they had forfeited. They remembered what it was like to have what they had given up. This is what human nature does to us. It always reminds us of the things we had when we don't have them any more. This is the essence of the attic:

• Just try to teach some new choruses, and you'll hear how great the hymns are.

• Try ministry with drama, and you'll hear how "we used to *preach* the Word."

• Try releasing others in ministry, and you'll hear about how "the *pastor* used to do the visitation."

• Try growing your attendance, and you will hear about when "we didn't use to compromise as a church."

• Try giving to missions, and you'll hear about how "we used to help our own."

• Try developing small groups, and you'll hear about how "we used to get together without having a plan."

• Try having a leadership retreat, and you'll hear how "we used to spend money on important things."

• Try multiple service times, and you'll hear about how "we used to know people."

No wonder our innovative pastors are tired! They're getting the "heaven" kicked out of them every day.

Sometimes I read books on church change and I think to myself, "I must have a different species of humans in my church than these other pastors do." I feel like every inch we take into the Promised Land comes with a couple of rounds' worth of bruises. I want to say to you, my pastor friends, that leading an established church through change is incredibly difficult. The attic issues jump out at you constantly. You are going to need the grace of God, the patience of Job, the commitment of Daniel, the fire of Elijah, and the determination of Paul.

66 You are going to need the grace of God, the patience of Job, the commitment of Daniel, the fire of Elijah, and the determination of Paul. **99**

Who among us has all of that? Please don't give up. Believe that God brought you to the church you are in to be a "change agent." You are reading this book for a reason. God is going to help you deal effectively with the attic issues of your church.

Every church has issues that need to be addressed. Some of these have been placed in the attic and left alone. The truth is that the church will not be able to move forward until it deals with the hidden issues in the attic. I remember asking about a particular family shortly after I started as pastor of my first church. I had a suspicion that there had been some problem because of the questions and actions the family pursued. I remember my dear friend on our deacon team asking, "Do you really want to know about that?" "Hmm," I thought, "maybe I don't." His question implied that the issues were sticky, muddy, and messy. This issue had been left alone and not completely resolved. It wasn't the deacon team's fault; they had tried to deal with it. It was just uncomfortable and challenging.

How many of those items can a church store in the attic? How many situations can we cram up into that attic and hope they go away? I've been a pastor long enough to realize the value of leaving certain things alone, but I've also learned that there are many issues we must not leave alone. Church leaders who refuse to deal with the attic will never really be ready or willing to face the changes necessary to move forward.

Let's consider some of the issues we may want to pull out of the attic and deal with.

CHURCH SECRETS

Many pastors have never taken the time to look into the past of the churches they lead. If you planted the church, you have a real advantage. You know the history, and you can make decisions based on that knowledge. However, many of the churches in our culture have histories the pastors know very little about. In some cases, it's difficult to find out your church's history. In other cases, that past needs attention.

When I came to Fort Collins, I did my research with some of the historians and charter members of our church. We walked through questions such as "Why did this church begin?" "What was the core group like and what was their purpose in starting this church?" "Where did they hold their meetings?" "What was a typical meeting like?" "How did the church impact the community?"

As these questions are asked, many things may begin to surface. A friend who did this discovered his church started from an "anger burst" during a business meeting. Some of the members walked out and decided to start their own church. This kind of beginning bred "bad blood" into all of the people who were part of this church. The church had a long history of fighting, bickering, comparing, and competing with other churches in the area. Their mission, without even their knowing it, was to overpower and overcome the other churches in the area. They measured their success by how much bigger they were than the church they had split from. What a tragedy. This spirit had to be dealt with.

Church secrets are sometimes the hidden issues that keep a church from being healthy. Church secrets create gaps between those who were involved in the church during the time of the secret and those who are new and know nothing about it.

A new Christian who is excited about ministry is perfect prey for the seasoned complainer who wants to quell his or her spirit. It only takes a few comments from the complainer to convince the new Christian that he or she is too idealistic and dreaming dreams that could never happen. The new Christian quickly learns to be still and stops taking risks that may make him or her appear foolish. I have experienced similar negativity from some pastors who are many years my senior. I remember a seasoned pastor who asked me to explain my vision for the church I pastor. I began to articulate some of the key components that make our church unique and specific in purpose. After listening to me for a bit, he shook his head and said something like "Oh, you young pastors live in such a fairy tale world." I was shocked and somewhat disappointed because this was a man that many respected and believed in.

In contrast to that experience, I had another conversation with a senior citizen who also had given his life to ministry. I shared similar visions and dreams with him, and I will never forget what he said to me. "Dary, that's the kind of vision that God will bring about and complete. Keep dreaming and pursuing that goal. God is able!" I left that moment feeling as though I was ten feet off the ground. I left believing that my God could do what he had planted in my heart.

The first pastor was remembering his past failures, and the second pastor was reflecting on his memories of success. Our faith seems to be tied closely to the outcome of our last risk. Church secrets seem to remain in the hearts of those who were involved, and it becomes increasingly more difficult for those people to believe God for significant success with similar risks.

If you launch a new visitation program in an established church, people will be quick to tell you about the success or failure the last time a similar ministry was launched. I've heard things from the "longevity" crowd in our church like "I'm not sure that we need a youth pastor." This was because they had a teenager who got crosswise with the last youth pastor. I knew nothing about that little secret. The longer a church has been around, the more little secrets and issues you have to overcome in leading them to new ground. The good news is that it can be done. The church I pastor was started in 1921. There are many little secrets and issues I've heard about over these years that I didn't ask to hear about. I've come to the realization that our church is writing our own secrets and history right now for the next generation of leaders.

COMPETITION

Churches that are driven by competition will never reach their potential. They only strive to reach beyond some other church's potential. If you're pastoring a church like this, you need to crawl around in the attic and find the source of the problem. Somewhere you'll discover the place and the time that this seed was planted in the heart of the church. These seeds are planted in a variety of ways. The seed may have been planted by a former pastor who wanted to prove something and created this competitive spirit in the church. If the church has a history of highly competitive pastors and other leaders, you'll need to address the issue head-on.

Here are some signs of a church that has a competitive spirit hidden in the attic:

• The people are bitter toward another church in town.

• People compare attendance numbers frequently to another church.

• Trophy racks all over the church boast of former victories.

• People have a superior attitude when their church is talked about publicly.

• Leaders don't demonstrate servant hearts.

• People don't want to clean up their own messes after using a room.

If you discover a competitive church spirit in your attic, you will need to begin praying, preaching, and teaching against it.

SENSATIONALISM

The spirit of sensationalism is a spirit that attacks a church from within. It's cultivated in the attic and released with a consuming need to control. You'll recognize this spirit by looking for the following things:

• A sound doctrinal principle will be exaggerated.

• Spiritual warfare principles will be taught with new non-biblical remedies.

• The dress code will be flashy.

• The church will not experience ecstatic joy when people accept Christ.

• Church members will take pride in being involved in something that feels "on the edge."

• Leaders will have very little true accountability.

This spirit is the spirit that came upon the church at Corinth. Paul tried to combat this spirit by instructing the Corinthians to do several things:

• Stop bickering over who you identify with most—Apollos, Paul, or Peter (1 Corinthians 1:12-17).

• Stop taking pride in things that should disgrace you (1 Corinthians 5:1-2).

• Stop using spiritual gifts as a means to promote yourself (1 Corinthians 14).

A church caught up in sensationalism forgets the basics of Christianity and reaches for something that satisfies the human nature. The visible, the touchable, the tangible, and the sensational become the pursuit of the church. God help us!

FEAR

It was fascinating to watch the Y2K phenomenon. I received at least a dozen books proclaiming that this was the end of the world in one form or another. I do believe a person with basic common sense should pay attention to potential glitches in technology; I'm not here to bash people who prepared themselves for a few bumps in the road. What concerned me was that so many Christians jumped on the bandwagon proclaiming the end of the world. I was criticized by some in our church for not preparing the church more adequately for this "dark hour."

No wonder we lose credibility among people we're trying to reach with the gospel. They see us as extremists. There is always some new bandwagon to ride that declares gloom, doom, and despair. I suppose we should get used to it, because it's not going to go away. People like to have a finishing point. People like to feel that they know when the end is going to come. How sad! When you motivate people through fear, you lose the opportunity to motivate them through and by love, because fear and love do not coexist. If you pastor a church that has been ruled through the years by a dominating fear, you need to preach and teach about God's peace and his plan.

GUILT

I've been in a few church services where they hang you over hell on a rotten stick. They turn up the thermostats and preach about hell for a solid hour. By the time they're done, you're convinced that there isn't anybody on earth that's going to heaven, especially you. Every church attic has a little guilt in it, but a guilt-driven church has a very unhealthy environment. People are paranoid and paralyzed. Many pastors resort to this method because it produces quick results. The problem is that the results have no lasting impact. People overcome the guilt and then struggle with anger at the person who put that guilt on them. It often causes people to go in the opposite direction. Warning people of the consequences of sin can bring healthy results. But healthy results can also come from teaching people that they can enjoy their relationship with God.

Here are some signs of a guilt-driven church:

• There are lots of altar calls and very little true discipleship.

• The church is focused inward and has very little community impact.

• Members demonstrate pride in how holy they are.

• The church embraces lots of rules and red tape.

If you pastor a church like this, help people understand their security in God. Provide ways for the church to experience some small wins before tackling something too big. Get them to look beyond their own salvation into the eyes of needy people. Begin praying from the pulpit for God's grace and mercy to release people from condemnation.

ACTIVITY

We live in a busy world. We find worth through being busy. We receive awards for being busy. People respect us if we convince them that we are truly busy. We are paid more if we are busy. Busyness fills the attic of most churches. After all, it's God's work, and we'd better be doing it. However, we don't always gain more ground by doing more. It would be wise for some of us to look through our bulletins and cancel about half of everything we do. (Please do not do that without careful thought.)

Have you ever tried to reach another busy pastor? If you have, you realize the similarity to the miracle at the Red Sea. We're busy people. We train our people to be busy, and we're headed for trouble. I really believe this is one of the ways Satan keeps us from doing the important things. Busywork may not be God's work.

A church that is driven by activity will suffer from many things, including:

• burnout,

• ineffectiveness,

• stress and depression,

• a lack of healthy relationships,

• quick-fix solutions to problems that require long-term remedies, and

• shallow training for leaders.

66 We need to lead our people to the streams of living water, not lead them over Niagara Falls. 99

97

Before we sign up our church people for another new program, let's have a season of rest. We need to lead our people to the streams of living water, not lead them over Niagara Falls.

There is a huge difference.

The Attic Issues of the Pastor's Personal World

We, as church leaders, have attics in our minds. The mind is a very strong, hidden place. I want to talk to you for a moment. I want to talk to the core of your heart. Don't continue reading this section right now if you don't have the time to read it slowly and carefully. It's the most important section of this book. I want to deal with your personal attic, that hidden place that no one dares to visit.

HIDDEN PAIN

We all have some type of hidden pain in our lives. This hidden pain affects our leadership roles and styles more than we might think. I'll lead the way by sharing with you some of my hidden pain.

When I was fourteen years old, my dad died of cancer. He was forty-one. I have four sisters; they were eighteen, sixteen, eleven, and nine when he died. I was in the middle. My mom was (and remains!) a very loving and godly woman. I respect her greatly. She helped us look to God as our Father throughout our childhood. My dad was a great man, and I loved him dearly. I was devastated by his death, and I lost a person of great influence in my life. I looked to God and trusted him to help me through this time. I never walked away from God, and I always believed God was with me through the lonely hours in my life. I did, however, build a shield in my life. It was a shield that protected me from intimacy and dependence on anyone else.

I grew up quickly since I was the only male in our household. Any time I got too close to someone, it seemed easier to end the relationship than to risk loving and losing them. I didn't realize how much this impacted my life. I had tons of friends, but no one that I could share with at the level I needed to share. It seemed like in the back of my mind there was a feeling that I would lose anyone who became special to me.

As I got married and had children, I've had to face this hidden pain. I've come to realize just how important it is to share my life with others. Primarily I share my life with God, but I also share with family and friends. My wife has helped me to tear down the wall of protection that I thought was keeping me safe all these years. With God's help, I'll continue to develop intimate relationships that are healthy and strong with my family and loved ones.

Hidden pain in the pastor's life is somewhat of a mystery. Pastors can't fully expose all of their issues to the churches they lead for fear of losing the confidence of others. Some people don't want to believe that their leader deals with ugly temptations just like they do. Your past is a very important component of your future. Your future is limited only by how well you deal with your past. The hidden pain in your personal life is something you need to understand and talk about. Once you've done this, you can move on to become a more effective leader. God will use your past hidden pain in powerful ways that you can't foresee. Give it to God!

PAST FAILURE

Past failure is different from hidden pain. Hidden pain may include a past failure, but past failure may not be part of your hidden pain. Past failure impacts our lives in the area of confidence. If you don't have the confidence in God to do what he has put in your heart to do, the leaders around you won't have confidence either. Your past failures, even if you don't remember them specifically, can work against you in the battle of self-confidence.

What does it mean to have God-confidence? God-confidence is that deep inner knowledge that God is big enough and great enough to do whatever the task will require. I have a very strong sense of God-confidence in my life. Most spiritual leaders do. The problem rarely lies in the confidence we have in God but rather in our self-confidence.

What does it mean to have self-confidence? Do names like Moses and Gideon come to mind? Both of these men had some real insecurity issues that they struggled with during their journeys with God. I believe self-confidence for the Christian is very different from self-confidence for the non-Christian. For the Christian, self-confidence remains related to God-confidence. We have this sense that if God has indeed called us to do this, then we can do it. Past failure impacts our leadership skills when we know God has called us to lead at a certain level, but we don't comprehend how we'll accomplish it. When I believe that God can do it and that God has called me to perform it but I don't have the confidence to try it, guilt emerges. I could tell you of so many times I asked the question, "Am I the right person to lead our church through this challenge?" In my spirit, I knew God was calling me, but in my flesh I knew I didn't have the ability it would take. I have made some strides in this area by doing the following things:

1. **Drawing closer to God.** You know the promise—if we draw close to him, he will draw close to us. This means more daily time listening, reading, and meditating on God.

2. **Writing out prayers.** This may seem strange at first if you haven't done it before. When you write out your prayers, you'll learn more about yourself than about God, and that's fine. You need to struggle through the concepts you are praying. Writing them down will force you to get more specific and contemplative. List your fears...there have been many times that the fears in my heart have been vague "feelings." When I tried to write them down, I discovered very few concrete fears to put on the page.

I remember teaching my horse to cross a creek. She was young and didn't have any experience in trail riding. In Colorado, you cross little creeks constantly. We came upon a creek that was about two feet wide. She was big and strong enough to walk right over that creek without even getting her feet wet.

However, she wasn't convinced that it would be that easy. She went back and forth, she hopped sideways to avoid going over the creek, and finally she tried to turn around and go the other way. This almost sounds like a guy named Jonah, doesn't it? Eventually my horse realized that I was requiring her to go over the creek. She came up to the edge and I could feel her legs and body begin to tremble as she began to pull herself together. Like a bolt shot up into the sky, she jumped as high and as far as she could. She cleared that creek by what seemed to be fifteen or twenty feet. We went back and did it again, and again, and again. Now, if my horse walked up to that creek, she wouldn't even stop walking as she went through it. Why? Because she no longer has the fear that was associated with the unknown.

Many times, our past failures create this unknown fear in us that needs to be conquered. Talk to someone you can trust and lay it all out there. Don't be afraid to share the issues of your heart with a person God has put in your life.

HABITUAL SIN

This is a tough one, isn't it? None of us ever struggle with the same sin over and over, do we? Maybe for the sake of discussion, we shouldn't call it sin, we should call it "our struggle."

The attic of our life is a very unique place. It remains as private as we allow it to remain. When sin enters our attic, it's usually because we didn't really want to remove it from the garage. We're forced to do one of two things with sin knocking on our door. We must either repent of it, which gets rid of it, or hide it, which places it up in the attic.

One of the elements that makes it attractive for the unchurched to poke around an open garage is the understanding of how we define and deal with sin. In our culture today, it's very awkward for unchurched people to hear us refer to them as "sinners." In their minds, that term is reserved for someone who has done something really, really bad. When they see and hear us talking about our desire to please God with the way we live our lives, it captures their attention. Remember this incredible story:

"The teachers of the law and the Pharisees brought in a woman caught in adultery. They made her stand before the group and said to Jesus, 'Teacher, this woman was caught in the act of adultery. In the Law Moses commanded us to stone such women. Now what do you say?' They were using this question as a trap, in order to have a basis for accusing him. But Jesus bent down and started to write on the ground with his finger. When they kept on questioning him, he straightened up and said to them, 'If any one of you is without sin, let him be the first to throw a stone at her' " (John 8:3-7).

I'm amazed at this story. None of these religious leaders could make claims about their own lives that they were expecting from others. They were the perfect example of a spiritual leader who keeps sin in the attic. It caused them to:

- judge others quickly,
- desire punishment rather than restoration, and
- leave the scene without taking proper action.

All three of these things are still done today. It's been interesting over the years to watch some of our spiritual leaders fall into immorality. Typically, we have seen one of two things: either they begin to preach against sin with a judgmental attitude, or they don't speak against sin at all and consequently they lose balance. They lose balance because their attics are filled with hidden sin.

When we hide our sin in the attic, it begins to impact our attitude toward sin, toward others, toward the world, toward God, but mostly toward ourselves. Living a double life is a miserable place to be. I want to recommend the following to you if you are entering into or have been living in this dilemma:

1. Set a date that allows you the freedom to start over. Make a vow to God that as of such and such a date, you will not engage in this sin again.

2. Decide beforehand who you'll talk with if the sin happens again. Write that name down and begin praying for that person to help you if you need help. If you can't think of someone you could do this with, pray that God would make it obvious to you who it might be. Make sure it is a trustworthy person of the same

sex. It may be that you'll need to travel to another city or state. Just do it.

3. If you participate in this sin again after the set date, follow through with the plan.

4. Draw up an accountability agreement and stick to it.

When you follow this plan, you'll be forced to get the sin out of the attic. Getting this into the open will release you to work on it with success.

As I've worked with pastors and Christian leaders, I have found several common sins that are hidden in the attic. I call them the "addicts of the attic."

• Sexual sin (pornography, adultery, and prostitution)
• Greed (gambling, stock market addiction, and overspending)
• Debt
• Jealousy (struggling with others who experience "success")
• Bitterness and resentment (perhaps due to unresolved conflict from years ago between the person and a denomination or a leader)
• Anger (perhaps directed at God for not answering a prayer "the way he should have")
• Pride (the need to appear bigger and better)

I hope you'll take this list seriously. When you open your garage for the unchurched to visit, you need to make certain that there is nothing hidden in the attic.

RISKS OF A FULL ATTIC

Fire

If you never clean out your attic, you have a greater risk of fire. That old dried-out stuff will become a potential hazard to you and your family. When your soul is dry and tired, you're at risk. Allow God to give you the strength to do what God does best—renew!

Wasted Space

When the attic is filled up with yucky stuff, it can't be filled up with good stuff. Don't waste away your potential. God has chosen you and given you this mantle of leadership for a reason.

God Cleans the Attic Eventually

God is patient but God will not be mocked. You will have your attic cleaned one way or another. My prayer for you is that you will partner with God and do a good job cleaning your attic. If you clean with him, he won't have to clean it without you.

Garage-Door Openers

1. Take a hard look at the attic of your personal life. What do you see?

2. Are you willing to invite someone to look around in the attic of your life with you? Set an appointment with that person this week to join you for an "attic tour."

3. Do you believe Christian leaders have a difficult time opening up to others with their personal issues? Why or why not?

4. How well do you know the history of the church you lead? Take the time to search through your history and discuss it with church leaders.

5. What are the characteristics that "drive" your church?

6. What "hidden pain" or "past failures" are keeping you from reaching your potential as a leader?

Chapter 6

The Concrete Floor:
PROVIDING A *SOLID* FOUNDATION FOR GROWTH

ew garages need carpet on the floor. The garage isn't a place for fine furnishings or delicate collectibles. There may be areas in a typical garage that are carpeted. For example, in our garage we have set aside a section for working out. We put down a piece of inexpensive carpet for warmth and comfort. But garages need to have concrete floors to support their practical and messy functions.

Churches need spiritual "concrete floors" to support healthy growth and development. Churches need concrete floors because:

- they're practical,
- they're easily cleaned up,
- they allow for movement,
- they're sturdy, and
- they can be added onto easily.

Let's talk through each of these reasons for having a spiritual concrete floor in your church.

Concrete Is Practical

Why go to the expense of placing carpet or oak flooring over an area that's used for parking a car or stacking up boxes? That would make no sense. We're living in an era of pragmatism. The challenges and deceptions of pragmatism are sometimes taken to extremes, but the church must find ways to live out its claims practically. When you begin to open the garage door to the unchurched of your community, you'll need to be practical.

> 66 When you begin to open the garage door to the unchurched of your community, you'll need to be practical. 99

I enjoy theology. It's a great adventure to open a good theology book, sip a cup of hot coffee, and work my way through new theological insights. It causes me to think about and examine my beliefs and convictions about God and myself. However, if I took pages from a theology book to the pulpit and read them aloud during one of our weekend services, many people wouldn't return the following week. Few unchurched people would even sit through such a thing the first time. They would struggle with a theology reading because they would sense no personal connection and they would glean no personal application. To them it would be just a bunch of words being read by some guy who thinks they matter.

People in our culture are used to things having practical applications—from computers to the drive-through windows of fast-food restaurants. Here are some areas in which you could become more practical.

SERMONS

Making the Bible applicable to people's "real" lives requires a working knowledge of "gaps." Let's explore some of the most prevalent gaps that pastors face.

The Generation Gap

It's a challenge to apply the Bible to people of varying ages. That's why so many generational churches have been birthed. They've chosen to reach one segment of people through certain methods and styles that appeal primarily to their target group. We're in the middle of planting such a church right now. However, even in a generational church, the variety of needs and understanding greatly varies.

We must learn to examine our sermons by asking questions like, "How will this message impact the seniors of our congregation?" "How will it impact the teenagers?" "What about the 'boomers' or 'busters'?"

I challenge you to try to develop language that resonates in the hearts of different age groups. For instance, if you're speaking on the life of Jonah, you may want to say something like, "How many of you teenagers have ever had a moment when you just want to do it your own way? Maybe you've gotten tired of someone else telling you what to do." They'll chuckle and raise their hands. Your next sentence may be, "How many of you experienced, seasoned adults sometimes feel like you've done your part and someone else needs to step up to the plate?" They'll nod their heads. Then you'll say, "Well, those may be some of the feelings Jonah had." You've just made a practical application to both the young and the old in your congregation. As you do this over and over in your message, you'll connect with your audience and speak practical truth to their hearts.

The Educational or Knowledge Gap

Not everyone in your congregation has the same amount of education or knowledge. Living in Fort Collins has presented this challenge to me in living color. Colorado State University is in our city. We have about twenty-three thousand students in our backyard. That means that we also have teachers, professors, and others with a high level of education. A sermon must apply to the intellectual thinker as well as to the person not involved in academics.

A few years ago, the teachers and professors in our church began coming together to exchange ideas and give support to one another. I once stopped in to say hello and discovered we had about six English teachers in our congregation. I jokingly asked them to keep me grammatically accountable through the years to come. Wow! Have they ever! I learned that one sentence with poor structure or grammar would distract these people. It's not that they're trying to be mean or judgmental; they simply know the proper way of saying what I'm trying to say.

You need to think of ways to reach the educated as well as the noneducated people of your community. Jesus was a master at this art. He could reach the intellectual and the simple in the same sentence. He could discuss the law with the Pharisee and the soil with the farmer. I'm not suggesting that you master all fields of knowledge. However, you must pay attention to and care about reaching people at different academic levels. Add a new word to your vocabulary once in a while. Challenge the thinker sitting in the congregation.

The Philosophical Gap

I received a letter this week from someone who was offended because I used humor during a sermon. This person believed that learning from the Bible was serious business and that humor made light of it. This person views ministry and preaching from a different philosophy or point of view than I do. Certain kinds of humor need to be rejected from healthy communication techniques, but I was not using inappropriate humor.

Other philosophical gaps exist in topics such as:

- ministry to the poor,
- tithing,
- drama,
- music,
- dress code,
- Bible translations,
- media,
- "big event" productions,
- ticket sales, and
- concerts.

People today have strong opinions about many topics. You must be ready to deal with different opinions in a constructive way. Don't get discouraged when someone disagrees with something you do. Find ways to work around the disagreement. Usually, for every one thing someone disagrees with you about, there are ten they agree with you about. Stay focused on the ten, and be open to dialogue about the one. You can't escape the philosophical gap, so don't try.

Recognizing and being sensitive to these gaps will help you connect to all kinds of people in preaching. Don't get locked into a narrow pattern of communication that only connects with one group. Strive to connect with everyone.

ADMINISTRATION

People in this culture don't want to face a lot of red tape or jump through a series of hoops to accomplish small tasks. Make it easy to get things done in your church. Communicate your process clearly. People feel comfortable and relaxed when they understand how the system works, even if they don't agree with it.

> **"People need to be comfortable with the process before they'll buy into the vision."**

There are entire books about how to manage a church. To dig deeper on this topic, I would encourage you to read a couple of them. I simply want to challenge you to look carefully at how the church you lead is administered. Does it make sense to the unchurched person? Does it make sense to the people who are in the church? People need to be comfortable with the process before they'll buy into the vision.

FACILITIES

When people enter a garage, they rarely need to be told, "This is the garage." The garage looks and feels so practical that there's little doubt you're in a garage. Here are a couple of practical suggestions to help make your facility practical:

Make sure traffic in the parking lot flows in an orderly fashion. This doesn't mean a person will always find a parking place, but it does mean that the person will be going the right direction in the parking lot. If it would help to have one-way lanes, paint arrows on the asphalt. Help people to feel like you're ready for them. Use parking lot attendants. This will help people see your efforts to assist them practically.

Have greeters at the door. Train greeters not to embarrass or overpower people as they come in. Some people want to come in without having to answer a list of questions from an aggressive greeter.

Provide a cry room. Parents with infants may want to participate in the service without worrying about their babies crying and disturbing others. But newcomers aren't always comfortable leaving their children in a nursery with unfamiliar staff. Sometimes it's just as worrisome for parents to leave their kids in a nursery as it is to keep them in the worship service. A great alternative is to provide a cry room that's visible to the worship area but separated by soundproof glass. Or you could broadcast the service by video into a detached room. Parents can sit in the cry room with their children without worrying about a thing.

Place signs up for guests. Someone who has never attended your church before should be able to find the restroom. Put up signs showing where to go for the nursery and children's ministry areas. A map of the facility would be helpful as well. Have ushers and greeters wear name tags so people will know who to ask if they have questions.

Provide quality printed materials. Provide a bulletin or order of service that gives people a practical guide to their experience at church. Make certain that the bulletin is easy to read and follow. This piece of paper may end up in their homes, reminding them of their experience at church. Make it meaningful and practical.

PEOPLE-FRIENDLINESS

Don't embarrass guests or well-known people. Some people enjoy being singled out, but the majority of people like to be left alone in a public setting. Respect their privacy.

We have the privilege of having a few well-known people in our church. These people don't want to be patronized by the pastor or anyone else.

Singling people out also causes others to mistrust you. They see you making a big deal out of other people's attendance but never mentioning theirs. I recently talked with an executive in our church about this very thing. He thanked me for allowing him and his family to be a part of our church without making a big deal out of it. Many people in our church work at the company he leads. I must balance my role as friend and pastor to all of these people.

MINISTRY

66 Provide ways for people to get involved quickly in meaningful ministry. 99

Provide ways for people to get involved quickly in meaningful ministry.

When new people get the impression they aren't qualified to do anything except sit and soak, chances are they will not stick around for long. There are lots of things newcomers can be involved in even though they aren't trained or members. They could paint a room in the church or clean up an area of your city. They could be parking lot attendants, sound technicians, or graphic artists. Find what people are good at and put their abilities to use in the church.

PARTICIPATION

Getting people involved through simple participation isn't difficult. By leading nonthreatening activities that somehow relate to the worship service, you are training people to be active learners. You could start by asking people to give their friends around them high fives or to say something as a group as you lead them. The key is to draw them into the worship experience by getting them to do something more than listening. Once they get involved, they'll relax and be less judgmental.

One way I draw people in is by including stories in my sermons that people in the congregation send me. Our congregation knows that I love to get e-mail with cute little stories and phrases. I get hundreds of them. I mention it often, and sometimes I'll get e-mail from first-time guests who want to share a story with me. It's simple and it doesn't violate their privacy or even reveal to me who they are. These are the kinds of stories I try to include in my sermons. I usually preach a series at a time, allowing people to send me information that fits the theme of an upcoming series. When I share these stories from the pulpit, those in the congregation feel like they're a part of the message—and they are.

Concrete Is Easily Cleaned Up

A concrete floor works well in a garage because it's so easy to clean up. If you've ever parked your car in the garage, you've probably had to clean up a few oil spots. A garage that's used will get dirty.

When a church opens its garage door, it attracts less-than-perfect people. People who will not come through the front door will come through the garage door of the church. The concrete floor puts them at ease. It's a safe place for them to make messes (or should I say, reveal their messes?). People in our world have many oil leaks, flaws, squeaky wheels, and broken parts. That's why they join twelve-step groups by the thousands—they have messes in their lives and need a safe surface to dump them on.

I visited an AA meeting recently near our church. I was invited by a group of bikers who attend Timberline, several of whom were attending the meetings to overcome alcohol addiction. I rode my Harley to the meeting, wanting to fit in. I drove into a parking lot packed with biker types (by the way, these are some of the nicest people you'll ever meet). The group standing outside looked me over and gave the nod that said, "Hey!" I greeted them with a loud, deep, booming, "Praise God, Brother" (just kidding). I greeted them with a simple nod and walked in only to find that the place was completely full.

It was graduation night. There were probably about 150 people crammed into this little tiny place. It was standing room only. I stood at the back as they started introducing the graduates one at a time. These were the people who had been alcohol- or drug-free for at least one year. They walked up to the front of the room, received their "one year sober" pins, and briefly shared their stories. I listened to the mess. People began to spill the oil all over the room. The pain and the honesty were refreshing; it was so safe, so real, and so raw.

> **"** When we open the garage door for lost, broken, wounded, and beat-up people, it'll be messy. It'll be ugly. It'll be hard. It'll take time, energy, and patience. It'll be difficult for church people to accept the mess, clean up the oil spills, and sweep up the dirt and grime that the world has poured out upon people. It'll require something of us; it'll cost us greatly. **"**

They all started their talks by saying their names and then a sentence I'll never forget. It went like this: "I'm an alcoholic and a drug addict. I've been drug- and alcohol-free for one year." The entire room would erupt with applause and cheers. It was like the introductions at the Super Bowl. Eyes were filled with tears. People shouted out encouraging words and lifted their arms, making fists as if to say, "You did it, man. You're my hero. I believe in you." I was stunned, and I couldn't move.

I stood in the back of the room as God changed my perspective. It was like I was standing in heaven looking at the overcrowded rooms of the world's rehabilitation centers on the earth below. I was weeping with joy until I looked into our churches and saw the empty altars, empty pews, and empty chairs. God allowed me to see just how religious and pious I had become. I felt as though God was looking right through me, asking and demanding, "Where is the mess in your church? Where are the multitudes that have found a concrete floor to bleed on? Where are the lost sheep that have no safety from the enemies of life? Where can they go to find acceptance and forgiveness? Where are the cheers of my people in celebration for a changed and transformed life?"

I was standing there alone, trying to catch my breath and force a smile onto my lips. A tear rolled down my face. "I am soooo sorry God," I prayed silently. I realized that the church needed to be perceived differently. Many of these people weren't interested in coming to church. They've been convinced that in church they can't bleed or spill oil on the floor.

In that moment, I came to a new understanding of opening the garage door. When we open the garage door for lost, broken, wounded, and beat-up people, it'll be messy. It'll be ugly. It'll be hard. It'll take time, energy, and patience. It'll be difficult for church people to accept the mess, clean up the oil spills, and sweep up the dirt and grime that the world has poured out upon people. It'll require something of us; it'll cost us greatly.

Our neat and tidy little Bible studies will be filled with repentant, emaciated people who will pour the pain out through their tears. Our dusted and decorated altars will be wept on, stained, and scarred. The black oil of sin will gush out over these altars as God cleans the souls of the unchurched. Our elegant stained glass windows will rattle with the cheers of the congregation lifting their voices in praise of a God who forgives the dark secrets of the past.

> " We have the broom and the rags, and God will provide the stain remover. "

My prayer has changed over these years. I have stopped praying for sermons that the religious would rate as a "ten." I have stopped wanting to please others and perform all the right duties. I now pray for God to send us the mess. We have the broom and the rags, and God will provide the stain remover.

Concrete Allows Movement

Have you ever tried to roll a cart or a wagon over a thick carpet? It doesn't work well. The wheels dig into the carpet, and the weight of the wagon increases the harder you push or pull. I fear that many churches are trying to move large loads of people over thick carpet, and they're getting stuck.

The people of this generation are ready to move. They've experienced change like no other in history. The changes that will occur in this nation during the next twenty years will be staggering. This week alone in our church, we had people in hospitals getting new knee joints, new hip joints, and new shoulder joints. Some people were getting parts put in, and others were getting a few things taken out. It's difficult to believe.

People are learning new skills at work every day. They're being challenged to use new computer software and new technology. Companies are growing at rates no one could have ever predicted.

Then there's the church: Same organ we had fifty years ago, "Blessssss Godah!" We've become change-resistant.

The concrete floor is a symbol that helps us understand flexibility. I can roll things around on the concrete in my garage. I can slide things around and rearrange things in a hurry if I need to. This is essential for new-millennium ministry.

A church that cannot adapt to change will not be effective in reaching the unchurched. I'm not talking about change that compromises the truth of Scripture or God. I'm talking about change that meets the needs of our generation. You must learn how to impact lives with the truth, or people will not be changed.

As you open the garage door to reach unchurched people, you'll need to be more flexible and mobile than the way you've done things in the past. Here are a few areas in which you could consider being more flexible:

• adding new service times that are more convenient for people in your area;

• discovering new methods of reaching groups of people in your area;

• creating media-driven services and chat-room classes;

• forming seeker groups, training groups, hobby groups, interest groups, medical groups, and political groups; and

• finding needs in your community you could meet that aren't being met by anyone else.

Go ahead and get radical. Do something that has never ever been done before. Make history.

Concrete Is Sturdy

Even though concrete allows flexibility, it also offers a solid foundation to place things on. The garage is the place that typically bears the weight of a family's heavy items—things like the van, the car, the bikes, the mowers, the weights, and the tools.

We live in a culture that offers little sturdiness and dependability. The church can make a difference in people's lives by offering a sturdy foundation for people to stand on.

It's strange to walk across a movable bridge. You can feel it move and swing to the rhythm of your cadence. It doesn't create a sense of security. People commonly bolt the last few feet just trying to hurry up to get across that type of bridge.

Insecurity and fear plague our culture. People are petrified to walk on bridges. But when they put their feet down on a solid piece of concrete, they feel secure and are willing to step further. We must get the garage door open so that people can walk across something solid rather than the swinging bridges of our culture.

We must answer the question, "How can we present this sturdy, solid foundation to our community?" Here are some answers:

Think community. I'm amazed at how many church leaders have never thought of ways to be involved in their communities. Offer your building as a shelter in case of emergency. Offer to be a voting site. Offer to be open for community meetings if your building can handle such a task. Offer your facility to mortuaries to hold funeral services in. Offer your facility for senior citizen events. Offer it for youth events or activities. Open it up for weddings.

I know what you're thinking: "Risk! Liability!" I know, I know. The point I'm trying to make is that you need to think bigger than your congregation. You need to think about your community. Does your community know you're there? Why or why not? Making your facilities available allows you to welcome people and let them step onto the concrete of your congregation's life. I can't begin to tell you the number of new attendees who have said to me through the years, "I attended a funeral at your church," or "I went to a wedding in your church once."

By thinking community, you can get people in the door who would never come to church otherwise—at least not yet! Once they come into the building itself, it becomes easier for them to come again. We have an attractive boardroom in our church with a nice table and comfortable chairs. I've offered that room to service clubs and other city groups. We've also provided snacks and drinks to them. It takes some work, but it's a way to get people to realize that you care about the community.

Let's bring this home even more. I encourage you to personally get involved in the community. Join a service club. Join a sports league or something that interests you. Coach your kids' team or someone else's kids' team. Go to community events like the symphony, plays, art shows, races, or whatever. Just get out from behind your desk and be visible in your community. You build a solid foundation for people to stand on when you invest time and energy in things besides building your church. Give some of yourself to your community, and the church you lead will become a sturdy foundation in your city.

Think longevity. You cannot build a solid, sturdy piece of concrete in a community in a short time. You'll need to be around long enough to weather some storms. Respect is usually earned over a long period of time. If you've soiled your reputation for whatever reason, you need to think about rebuilding it or leaving town. When you establish yourself in a long-term capacity, you become a reason for people to step into the garage.

Another key to building a sturdy floor is trust. Does the church you lead have a reputation for being trustworthy? Do you do what you say? Do you pay your bills? Do you have high ethical standards? Are you willing to help others through their pain?

Our mission statement is "Let Love Live." This is more than a statement. We're giving our all to live those words. To let love live, we need to be deliberate and skillful with our actions. We must understand that this mission requires accountability and visibility. Trust is one way to measure success. To establish trust with your community, you must *be* a trustworthy community.

Concrete Can Be Added Onto Easily

One of the best things about concrete is that it can be added onto without a lot of difficulty. Just clear the way and pour some more cement. A church that opens the garage door for the world to enter will experience incredible growth and expansion.

> 66 A church that opens the garage door for the world to enter will experience incredible growth and expansion. 99

Let me tell you a little bit about my journey of adding concrete. I've been through some exciting and trying days of expansion. We've gone from holding one weekend service to currently having five. We need to add one more as I write this. Please don't think that I'm proud or arrogant about our growth. I'm actually scared to death most of the time. I'm a first-time senior pastor with no experience in any other church this size. We're learning as we go.

Timberline has grown from about 150 people to around 3,500 people attending on a weekend. It's taken fourteen years to reach this level. The church has been in Fort Collins for over eighty years. We have a great heritage, and we are making a mark in Northern Colorado. I say all this to let you know that I have learned through some humbling mistakes how to add concrete to the garage floor.

As you add to your concrete floor, don't be afraid. The more you use the garage, the messier it will get. Don't expect to have a designer garage that everyone wants to take photos of. As more and more people come and spill oil on your floor, the less attractive it will be to those who just want to have a clean garage. But trust me, the people you invite to spill their messes on your floor will be eternally grateful that you stopped worrying about image and started caring about touching their hurting lives. Your concrete floor reveals your priorities.

Garage-Door Openers

1. What points challenge you the most in this chapter? Why?

2. Look back over the last two sermons you've preached. What practical applications have you asked for?

3. What are the "red tape" issues that frustrate you or your staff? How can you simplify these areas?

4. List ways people can get involved quickly in the ministries of the church you lead.

5. Are you comfortable around messy, hurting people? Why or why not? How does your attitude enhance or minimize your ability to open the garage door?

6. In what ways have you become involved in your community outside the role of being a pastor? What new areas could you become more involved in?

Chapter 7

The Mousetrap:
PUTTING A STOP TO THE NEEDLESS MESS

A mouse is a little gray creature that gets into the garage and leaves behind a trail of droppings, a filthy mess, destruction, odor, and frustration. Similarly, a church mouse is anything or anyone that leaves behind a trail of droppings, a filthy mess, destruction, odor, and frustration.

Spotting the Mouse

When I was dating my wife Bonnie, my sister Angie and her husband Greg invited us over for dinner. They lived in a small downstairs apartment; it was old and had been through a few remodeling programs. My sister is an outstanding cook, and we were looking forward to an enjoyable evening and a great meal.

We were gathered in the kitchen just before the food was to be served. We were talking and laughing, having one of those pleasant nights of fun. All of a sudden, we saw what appeared to be a bolt of lightning going across the kitchen floor. It looked like it was going a hundred miles an hour. There was no sound, no warning, no time to prepare for the shock.

My sister and Bonnie climbed up the wall toward the table like they had received a 220-volt electrical shock through their bodies. It was like one of those movies in which people can walk sideways on walls. It seemed like all of this happened in a split second. Initially there were no words, only the sound of chilling screams. Then someone screeched, "A mouse!" We all knew it was a mouse, but we needed to swallow our stomachs before speaking it out.

Suddenly our dinner plans were of no great importance. We had a mission to accomplish. We had passion. We had found a purpose worth fighting for. It was our call of duty to save and protect our loved ones from this attacker.

In unity, Greg and I proceeded to gather our combat gear from different places in the kitchen. He found a stick, and I found a broom handle. These lethal weapons were going to be used for intense war. Our eyes were wide, our teeth were closed tightly together, our faces were hard, and our bodies were trembling. The adrenaline was thick in our blood, and we committed ourselves fully to the process.

Bonnie and Angie were holding and comforting each other through the pain and terror of this traumatic moment. Greg and I marched to the refrigerator, under which the mouse had tried to hide himself from two of the greatest mouse-chasers this world has ever known. We nodded at each other, and Greg took the lead. He pulled the refrigerator away from the wall while I looked behind it. We were holding our weapons in ready position.

"I see the tail," I screamed out. "Back me up," I said as I advanced into a position of attack. Just before I could get my broom handle on the mouse, it bolted back across the room. This time the mouse had to dodge the fire of broom handle and stick coming down like torpedoes all around it. The noise was almost unbearable to Bonnie and Angie. They held their ears as the sounds of war filled the house.

Under the table, then across to the trash can, over to the front of the sink cabinet—this mouse was seriously messing with our party. Finally, with one sweeping blow, the battle came to an end. The mouse had met its match. It lay there, dead. It was no longer a threat. We mounted its head in the living room as a warning to all other mice (just kidding). The threat was over.

I think of this story when I'm in the middle of trying to find the church mouse. The church mouse can come out of nowhere at lightning speed. Just when I think all is well and that we're on track as a church, the phone rings or I find that little note on my desk that's folded up and taped and says "Personal" on it. Or my secretary says, "I need to talk to you about this phone call I got."

The church mice show up from time to time without much warning. Sometimes you actually see them scurry across the room. Other times, you only find the droppings they've left behind: hurt, pain, disunity, confusion, frustration, anger, strife, and judgment.

The garage is no place for a mouse. There are too many things they can get into and leave a stench. How can we, as church leaders, address the problem of church mice? I'm convinced that if we don't go to war against these little culprits, they'll scare away many of the people who are interested in coming into the garage.

Church mice gossip, buck the system, undermine leadership, and cause disunity. They're the ones who inform newcomers of all the "bad" stuff the pastor has done. They're the ones who "down talk" the church at every opportunity. They're the ones who think they could do a better job running the church than the current leadership and let others know that fact.

When unchurched people see mice, they run away as fast as they can. They jump onto the workbench and look for a safe way to exit. We need to develop healthy ways to catch these mice before they damage the body.

> 66 When unchurched people see mice, they run away as fast as they can. They jump onto the workbench and look for a safe way to exit. 99

Setting the Mousetrap

Remember the old game called Mousetrap? It was fun to play because it had a long, involved process at the end of which a mouse was finally trapped. A ball rolled down a rail and into a pail. The drop caused a diver to splash into a cup, bringing a trap down from the top of a tower to land on top of the mouse.

In my garage, it's a little different from that. I've found the spot where the mice usually come from. This is important because it allows me to set the trap in the right place.

But how can we find the mice in the church? Here are several ways:

Be approachable as a pastor or leader. When you're willing to talk about issues without getting overly defensive, people will share thoughts and concerns with you. This allows you to get ahead of the mice. I've talked with many pastors who could have kept the mice away but didn't take the concerns of others seriously. People who share concerns with you may be the best friends you have.

> 66 People who share concerns with you may be the best friends you have. 99

Sometimes just listening to people's concerns will keep them from leaving their droppings in the garage. Create an effective way to get feedback from people. You could include a communication card in the seat backs, establish an e-mail address where people can send concerns, or host a pastor's chat night. Be sure to follow up quickly on people's ideas and concerns.

I'm not suggesting that you create more avenues and ways for people to complain. I'm simply asking you if you currently have any open communication avenues. I talked to a pastor recently who told me he didn't have any problems in his church. He told me that if people didn't like it, they could leave. The problem was, they did—almost all of them left. I believe that many of these people were good people with good hearts. When you don't give people an opportunity to communicate their feelings to you, you're inviting the mice into the house. Be approachable!

Develop trust with your leadership teams. Not every problem you have needs to go in front of your board or leadership team. What's important is to create an environment that places a high value on church health.

> 66 If you respond in anger, it's you that's allowing the mouse to run through the house, not them. 99

Loyalty comes as a result of long-term trust and understanding. You cannot expect to be trusted if you're not trustworthy. The people around you need to see your trustworthiness and your desire to share the vision with them.

Discuss issues openly with your leaders. When your leadership team watches you strive for and desire church health, they'll value it as well. This empowers other leaders to share with you the unpleasant things they know about. If you respond in anger, it's you that's allowing the mouse to run through the house, not them. People should not be afraid to bring you bad news.

A member of our leadership team came to me once explaining this very thing to me. He said it was difficult to bring bad news to me because I was such a positive person and liked to keep things upbeat. I talked with my wife and a few close friends about this. It was unanimous: I was guilty. I had to relearn how to respond to bad news. I still don't like bad news, but I refuse to take it out on the informant. I'm learning to express thankfulness to people for being concerned enough to share it with me. I may be happy for a while with my head in the sand, but I certainly will not be effective.

Ask direct questions of people who express concerns about issues at church. While writing this chapter, I got a phone call from one of our pastors. He said that there was something I would want to know about. Here we go! A family in our church is considering leaving. They came into his office yesterday and told him why they were thinking of changing churches. Sound familiar? The reasons go something like this:

- "We're just not getting fed here."
- "This church doesn't confront sin enough."
- "The weekend services are geared too much to unchurched people."

These words hurt. They're painful. I began to ask for specifics to find out why they would make these statements. I don't believe these statements are true, but I asked specific questions to gain an understanding about this perception. Did I resign over it? No. Did I stop writing this chapter because I'm discouraged? No (my editor would have killed me). Did I respond in love and seek to find details? Yes.

Go ahead, ask people to explain why they feel the way they do! Ask them why they like or don't like certain things! Step out of your safe zone and face some of the things you don't want to face. Why? Because it will make you a better leader and pastor!

> 66 Step out of your safe zone and face some of the things you don't want to face. Why? Because it will make you a better leader and pastor! 99

Multiplying Mice in the Church

Mice multiply more quickly in certain environments than in others. Although it's virtually impossible to eliminate all mice, there are ways to minimize them. Let's talk about the kinds of churches that are fertile breeding grounds for church mice.

CHURCHES THAT ARE INWARDLY FOCUSED

People in inwardly focused churches have made a commitment to each other and don't even realize that outsiders don't feel welcome. It's the classic example of a new family coming in and sitting down, only to have a regular attendee tell them to move over because they're in his or her seat. This is a revealing moment for the guests. They've just caught a whiff of a mouse. It's unpleasant and very alarming. It frightens the newcomers, and they may bolt onto the workbench just to find an exit.

Inwardly focused churches usually don't even know they're inwardly focused. Pastors who are inwardly focused often don't know it either. They will not even be reading this book. Hopefully you're reading this book because you want something more than you have. You're searching for ideas and ways to be more effective in a changing world. You're to be commended.

Make certain you evaluate the ministries in your church often enough to stay outwardly focused. Be strategic. Be a thinker. Be aware. Unchurched people don't want to be a part of a little church club. They want to be a part of something that's big enough to change the world. When they come into your garage, make sure they see the big picture and not just the mouse.

> 66 Unchurched people don't want to be a part of a little church club. They want to be a part of something that's big enough to change the world. 99

CHURCHES THAT DON'T GIVE

Mice multiply when there's trouble with a church's financial support. I realize that you'll probably always need more money, but I want to address a deeper issue. When the money isn't coming in like it once was, we tend to go out there and tell people to give more. We build a sermon series around good stewardship and all that stuff. Don't get me wrong; I preach those series and believe in challenging people to give, too. However, the first question we should ask is, "Why isn't our giving growing?" A healthy church should have a growing budget if it isn't in an economically challenged area. I've discovered that a lack of giving happens when the following things happen:

• **People forget the vision.** People will not give if they don't understand or believe in the church's vision. You need to remind people of your vision at least once every thirty days. Answer the question, "Why are we doing what we're doing?" People will continue to share their resources if they believe they're making a difference.

Remember the game Tug of War? People on each side hold onto opposite ends of the same rope and begin to pull. The side that first starts gaining ground usually wins because people pull harder when they sense they're winning. When people sense they're winning and giving to a winning cause, they'll give more.

> **66** When people sense they're winning and giving to a winning cause, they'll give more. **99**

• **People don't see the results.** This point parallels the point above. Find ways to share the miracles within your congregation. Show people the situations through which others have experienced God's faithfulness. You could have a quick, five-minute spotlight of God's love shared by people in the congregation. You could show video clips of people who've experienced "wins" in their personal lives. You could tell stories of God's hand in healing broken relationships. Little things like this can ignite a church toward giving because they see the result of the ministry they're supporting.

Why should we let every other organization tell people success stories? We often lose financial gifts because people find more fulfillment giving to organizations that tell them where their money is going and what it's doing. You can catch the mouse if you'll begin to show people what they're supporting and the difference they're making.

A few months ago, God impressed upon my heart to take an offering during our weekend services for three smaller churches in our city that are trying to expand. We are in the middle of a significant relocation project ourselves and didn't have the money to do this. But I felt like God wanted our church to experience the joy of giving to others before we give to our own project.

We announced the plan. People responded and gave abundantly. It killed the mouse of selfishness. We announced the totals, and people in the church applauded what God had done. People loved listening to the cards of thanks from these other churches in town, not because of pride, but because they saw the reward of their sacrifice.

CHURCHES THAT HAVE DISUNITY

Visitors have a keen awareness of the unity or the lack of unity in the garage. They can smell the mouse of disunity almost before they walk in the door. I don't want to create a church of uniformity. That would be boring! Unity isn't uniformity, but rather, diversity with cooperation. If the church lacks unity, the world will have no desire to be a part of it.

> 66 Unity isn't uniformity, but rather, diversity with cooperation. 99

I'm encouraged that Jesus struggled with the unity of his own handpicked team. Mark 9:33-37 tells of one of these times:

"They came to Capernaum. When he was in the house, he asked them, 'What were you arguing about on the road?' But they kept quiet because on the way they had argued about who was the greatest. Sitting down, Jesus called the Twelve and said, 'If anyone wants to be first, he must be the very last, and the servant of all.' He took a little child and had him stand among them. Taking him in his arms, he said to them, "Whoever welcomes one of these little children in my name welcomes me; and whoever welcomes me does not welcome me but the one who sent me.' "

I really love reading stuff like this because it gives me hope. If Jesus struggled to keep unity on the team, so will we. This is a constant battleground for the church of the new millennium.

When unchurched people come into the garage and catch a glimpse of the mouse of disunity, they'll doubt our integrity. I've seen more unity in non-Christian businesses than exists in many churches proclaiming the good news of Christ. The unchurched expect unity, and they should. We'll never be perfect, and I realize the unity issue requires tremendous work and commitment. But I desire to see spiritual leaders accepting the responsibility to care passionately about church unity. It's one of those items we're afraid to address or we only address when there's a problem.

> 66 We need to work harder and smarter by maintaining church unity rather than fighting for it after we've lost it. 99

I change the oil in our automobiles every three thousand miles. I have determined not to wait until the car blows up to get this done. Similarly, we need to work harder and smarter by maintaining church unity rather than fighting for it after we've lost it.

Talk from the pulpit about the need to walk in unity. Describe what unity means to you. Describe what you believe the Bible says about it. Tell stories about maintaining unity in the church you lead. The people will learn to be jealous for church unity only if you are.

If I sense the mouse of disunity in our church, I do the following:

- I discuss my concerns and the issues with our pastoral team.
- I discuss my concerns and the issues with our leadership team.
- I determine whether others share the same concerns.
- I explore what issues have been raised and whether they need to be addressed. If others don't feel my concerns are an issue, I relax and try to forget them.
- I confront, or have someone confront (depending on the department and the need) the person or people one-on-one. This allows the opportunity to do healthy fact-finding about what was actually said or done. If this doesn't resolve the matter, the other people affected should be brought into the discussion.
- I pray through all these processes. Prayer changes and prepares me.

CHURCHES THAT ARE PREOCCUPIED WITH "BUSINESS"

Think of the classic story of Mary and Martha in the Bible. Mary is sitting at the feet of Jesus, and Martha is in the kitchen working and preparing the meal. When Jesus applauds Mary for her worshipful heart, he implies that Martha missed the mark. The question remains: Was there value in what Martha was doing? After all, someone needs to be preparing and working toward the goals of the church.

The point Jesus makes is that there's a time for everything. Worship should be at the top of the list. The other functions of church life can be considered "ministry" only if the priority of exalting Christ remains foremost. We often prioritize the "ministries" concept over the "exalting Christ" requirement.

> **❝** When the goal of the people in the church is to do more for God rather than to be in relationship with God, you've created an opportunity for the mouse to leave his droppings throughout the garage. **❞**

As a church leader, I set goals for attempting to involve people in meaningful ministry. Thus, people sometimes get the idea that being involved in a specific ministry is more valuable than being involved in exalting Christ. When the goal of the people in the church is to do more for God rather than to be in relationship with God, you've created an opportunity for the mouse to leave his droppings throughout the garage. Business-oriented churches emphasize "doing" rather than "being." There are a couple of ways to tell if your church has fallen into the business trap:

• **People are getting burned out.** Burnout happens when the plate of responsibility is fuller than your soul. It's that simple.

• **People are getting resentful.** Martha was resentful because she was doing all the work and no one else cared to help. People who work hard in the church easily become focused on what others are not doing. The attitude of "Why can't someone else do something around here?" is a mouse that eats away at the joy of serving.

Identifying Mouse Holes

I've discovered several places in my garage where mice enter. They enter through those places because of a crack in the concrete, a gap in the door, or a hole in the siding. It's not enough for me to simply acknowledge that these are the places where they enter; I must do something about it. Failure to block the hole or fill the gap allows mice to keep coming in through that spot. I may destroy the mice that have entered, but I'll be frustrated over and over if I do nothing about the entry point.

I recently filled a gap between the concrete and the wall where the concrete had settled over the years. When I finished the job, I smiled as if to say, "Try to get in here now, you little mouse."

Building effective ministries in a church requires you to block the pathway of the mouse. When you deal with these gaps and cracks, you show your commitment to preventing the mice from harming anything in the garage. You need to put more of your energy toward preventing mice issues than catching mice.

A good rule in your ministry may be that after you catch the mouse, you'll commit yourself to finding the place it entered and blocking that pathway. When people see you putting energy into preventing mice issues, they'll join you in the cause. The declaration of war against church mice should not be "Let's catch and destroy" but "Let's catch, destroy, and prevent more mice from entering."

> **66** A good rule in your ministry may be that after you catch the mouse, you'll commit yourself to finding the place it entered and blocking that pathway. **99**

I recently blocked up a mouse entry-point in our church. I received a letter from someone who had visited our church and checked the box on the communication card asking for more information about a certain ministry. She received nothing. This created frustration and confusion, resulting in her talking to others (you get the picture). I simply asked the ministry leader what had happened, and he said he never received the card with that request.

Long story short, we had a quick, five-minute meeting to resolve the issue and get back on track, ensuring this would not happen again. Had we ignored the issue and passed it off as though it was the visitor's problem, we would have allowed other mice to enter through that same hole. Make a commitment right now that you will not ignore issues that need to be dealt with.

Here are some common holes through which mice get into churches:

POOR STRUCTURE

I can talk about this mouse with great confidence. I've battled this little guy for many years. At Timberline Church, we've faced so many restructuring issues that I sometimes think I would love an eight-to-five, ho-hum, routine job.

This particular mouse is rarely caught in time. Changes in church structure are necessary when a church experiences growth. And when a church isn't experiencing growth, it may be because of poor structure. It's a double ring that must be thought through carefully.

The structure of the church is similar to the skeletal system of the body. Imagine yourself now without any bones. You would be reduced to a bag of stuff lying on the ground trying to ooze your way through life. Not a pretty picture. The bones give you the ability to move and the ability to balance and enjoy life. Proper structure in the church gives you the same.

I like what Bill Hybels said, "There is nothing like the local church when the local church is working right." Poor structure will keep a church from working right. Proper structure will help a church function according to its purpose.

> **66** Changes in church structure are necessary when a church experiences growth. And when a church isn't experiencing growth, it may be because of poor structure. **99**

But how do you know if the structure is working and when it may need to change? Workshops and books can help you discover proper structure for the church you lead. However, most of the changes we implement in our structures come as a result of one of the following three things:

• **A leadership need.** This is the easiest to detect. A certain ministry has grown to a place where it needs greater release or overseeing in order to remain effective. Changes in leadership and structure of this ministry are needed in order to keep it fruitful.

• **A breakdown in communication.** If you're struggling over the same stuff several times during each staff meeting, something is wrong. Healthy communication can only come if the lines are clearly established. As I am writing this, there's a war going on between a major phone company and many users in the Denver area. The phone company promised to provide service. But people wanting phone service are waiting up to four months to get it. This is a constant grind to those waiting. Every time they need to make calls from their new homes, they're faced with this same challenge and frustration, over and over and over.

I believe churches go through this same dilemma. People expect you to carry through on your promises. When you have a breakdown in the lines of communication, it creates a new mouse in the garage. People seem less patient than they used to be. As a church leader, you need to find multiple ways to communicate with people. You can use letters, fliers, bulletins, inserts, postcards, phone calls, and e-mail. You must learn to respond rapidly to the needs before you.

At Timberline we do all we can to keep everyone on the same page. If you have a church service planned that involves an awesome sermon, an awesome special song, awesome worship, and an awesome drama, yet you do not plan a good structure flow for the service, it won't be so awesome. You must communicate the right message with the right method at the right moment.

> 66 You must communicate the right message with the right method at the right moment. 99

- **Specific ministry focus.** If God begins to give you a vision for something new (I hope he does this often), you'll need a structure to help you realize this vision. A church that decides to start a Christian school needs to look very closely at the structural changes needed to launch it successfully. If you're considering starting a new worship service at a new time, you'll need to be realistic about the demands this will create. Structural change will be essential to maintain effectiveness.

SATISFACTION

One of the causes of mice in the church happens when you and other leaders become satisfied with the number of people already in the garage. Please understand that I believe in biblical contentment. I also believe in aggressively doing all we can to grow and develop the churches of which we are stewards. I've watched over the years as some pastors have become satisfied with the churches they pastor—decent salary, good ministry, healthy staff, enough people to enjoy without being overworked or burdened. This causes a real dilemma.

A few years ago, my wife and I purchased an older home. We decided it would be a good "fixer-upper." It was. The process taught us many things. Don't worry, I won't bore you with all the details.

We had some serious mice problems in this house and thought a cat would be the perfect remedy. We answered an ad in the paper and brought home a black Persian longhair feline.

A few days later, Bonnie and I witnessed something we couldn't believe. This cat was sitting next to a vent waiting for a mouse to enter. We watched as the mouse came up through the vent and ran across the room. To our amazement, though, the cat just stared at it. The mouse crossed the room several times and literally was within a few feet of the cat. But the cat had no interest, no appetite, and no desire.

The cat was satisfied she would get her food from a little paper bag and a nice kitty dish. She never made one move toward the mouse. She didn't accept the fact that this was her role in our home. She had limited her role to sitting, lying down, stretching out, yawning, eating, and sleeping. That was it. She was satisfied with her life the way it was and was determined not to leave that satisfaction circle. I have met a few pastors like that.

Usually, dealing with mice is messy and risky. A satisfied pastor who is a few years away from a good retirement doesn't want to mess anything up. "Why go after this mess? It was here when I came; it'll be here when I leave." I would like to say, "It better not be."

My favorite time in the life of Timberline Church was when the church had grown from around 150 to about eight hundred. At that point, I had staff, secretaries, accounting, janitorial help, and a good solid relationship with almost everybody in our church. It was fabulous. I could name the family, the kids, and even the dog. I felt like it could never get better. I was fulfilled and empowered. I had time and energy. I was creative and could manage the responsibilities in my life. I liked it. It was comfortable. I was satisfied. But I truly believe today that if I had continued to hold on to the ministries I enjoyed so much, our church would have never experienced the changes that God had in store for us.

Frustration came as I learned to release ministry, responsibility, and authority. This was not comfortable or as fulfilling to me personally. I needed to let my personal preference and personal fulfillment take a back seat to the advancement of God's church. It was difficult and stretching.

> 66 I truly believe today that if I had continued to hold on to the ministries I enjoyed so much, our church would have never experienced the changes that God had in store for us. 99

Over the next few years of growth, I found myself having to release some of the things I loved most. I could no longer do the weddings, funerals, dinners, graduations, and social stuff. It was a big adjustment. I can honestly tell you that I am more fulfilled today than ever—not because I'm doing what I like most, but because I committed myself to being personally obedient to God. I left the self-satisfaction trap and journeyed to higher ground.

I'm so glad that our Lord went through the Garden experience. He drank the cup. He left the personal-satisfaction experiences behind him and climbed the grueling Mount Calvary. His purpose was greater than being personally satisfied.

Even in his question to his father about finding some other way to accomplish the task of redemption, Jesus recognized the need to obey and face death on the cross. Wow! What a shepherd! What a pastor!

I hope you will not misunderstand my heart. I believe you should find true fulfillment in the calling God has placed on you. However, your calling will lead you beyond personal satisfaction—into utter dependence, complete emptiness, brutal soul-searching, and unspeakable joy.

> **Your calling will lead you beyond personal satisfaction—into utter dependence, complete emptiness, brutal soul-searching, and unspeakable joy.**

COMFORT

I have the privilege of having a heated garage in my current home. It's wonderful. We have some cold days and nights here in Colorado. It's comforting to walk out into the garage and enjoy the warmth.

This heated garage, however, attracts mice from outside the walls. They feel the heat. They want the heat. Therefore, they work hard to find a way to get into my garage.

A church that's warm and inviting attracts a certain brand of people that, shall I say, could be related to the mouse family. It's cold out there in the world. There's little heat and warmth available.

This relates to the issue of transfer growth. People coming from other fellowships need a home and will be a great help to the ministries of your local church. However, at times you must be cautious.

We've tracked our growth for the last eight years. We've discovered that we grow in three ways. Thirty percent of our church growth has come from people who move into our community. We are blessed with a strong economy and a growing population. Forty percent of our church growth comes from people accepting Christ into their lives. The other thirty percent of our church growth comes from transfers from other local congregations.

One of the reasons these people are coming and getting involved is that we're a warm and friendly group of people. Timberline is a healthy place to worship God. We have a good reputation in our community, and people know about us.

> 66 I'm concerned about those who have a history of being church mice in other fellowships and who are coming to our church to continue the destruction. 99

Here's the problem: some of our church transfers are leaving the churches they've belonged to because of discipline issues. This isn't always the case. People change churches for good reasons as well. Perhaps they've been unjustly hurt or misled. We should open our door widely in these cases. Fortunately, I have a great relationship with other pastors in our community, and I can find these things out when necessary. I'm concerned about those who have a history of being church mice in other fellowships and who are coming to our church to continue the destruction.

What are the implications of making it too comfortable for the mice? Do you follow my concern here? There are times we need to go to the mice and address the same issues that caused them to leave their previous fellowships. I make a habit of calling the former pastor of people who start attending our church when I suspect that there may be a problem. I don't think I would appreciate my neighbor trapping the mice in his garage and then bringing them into my garage and turning them loose. Yet, that's often what we do when it comes to discipline issues in the church.

On one occasion, I asked a family to come in and meet with me about their previous experience at another church in our town. I knew their former pastor well and had heard his side of the story. As they began to explain their situation, they were unkind and mean-spirited in their comments about their previous pastor. I knew the day would come when they would be saying these things about me. I decided it might as well be sooner than later.

I confronted them and asked them to apologize to their previous pastor and the church leaders. Believe it or not, they did. God brought them to a new place of understanding; they began to see the bigger picture of the Kingdom of God.

Not all my stories like this one end so happily. There have been times in which we have had to ask the transplanted mice to leave. I hope you understand my point in all of this: a warm, loving church is an open door for people who have been hurt and wounded in another church environment. This is a good thing. But be careful not to make destructive people so comfortable that they fill your garage.

Catching the Mouse

How you catch mice in the church says a lot about your leadership style. Let's examine a couple of methods for catching the church mouse.

THE D-CON METHOD

This method is accomplished by feeding the mice something that kills them. Follow me on this one. Some people have never been a part of a healthy church environment. When you bring good food to the pulpit and nourish people's souls to a place of contentment and growth, the old mouse spirit dies away.

> **When you bring good food to the pulpit and nourish people's souls to a place of contentment and growth, the old mouse spirit dies away.**

Jesus practiced this often. The fifth chapter of Matthew is filled with d-Con. Christ's words are poisonous to a mouse spirit:

"You have heard that it was said, 'Love your neighbor and hate your enemy.' But I tell you: Love your enemies and pray for those who persecute you, that you may be sons of your Father in heaven. He causes his sun to rise on the evil and the good, and sends rain on the righteous and the unrighteous. If you love those who love you, what reward will you get? Are not even the tax collectors doing that? And if you greet only your brothers, what are you doing more than others? Do not even pagans do that?" (Matthew 5:43-47)

Jesus had the ability to offer food to the hungry that destroyed the appetites of the flesh. We must do the same.

THE MOUSETRAP METHOD

This is the good old-fashioned way of handling the mouse. I have several mousetraps in my garage that I keep in a drawer. Whenever I see the signs of mice in the garage, I know it's time to set the trap. I place a little cheese on the metal bait-spot and flip the lever over the spring. I place it in the right spot and wait until morning.

The time will come when you'll be able to lovingly confront (trap) the mouse with the details of the situation at hand. Be firm and kind. The mousetrap is painful. But sometimes there's no other way. It should happen carefully and quickly.

Jesus let the mousetrap snap one day as he traveled through the Temple area. Matthew 21:12-13 tells us about it:

"Jesus entered the temple area and drove out all who were buying and selling there. He overturned the tables of the money changers and the benches of those selling doves. 'It is written,' he said to them, ' "My house will be called a house of prayer," ' but you are making it a 'den of robbers.' "

66 You don't need to apologize for holding the standards of God in high regard. 99

Jesus wasn't trying to show everybody how powerful he was. He was merely trying to protect something that was sacred. You should never enjoy setting the trap and flexing your muscles so that others realize how much authority you have. But you must hold people accountable for their actions and attitudes. You don't need to apologize for holding the standards of God in high regard. Jesus made a whip and went to work. I never want to enjoy that part of my responsibility; I do, however, want to be faithful to that responsibility.

Bringing It Home

Take a few moments right now and examine your own heart. These next few sentences may be difficult, but please read them with an open mind. This has to do with you, your thoughts, and your decisions.

Sometimes, as a pastor, I turn into a mouse myself. I don't do this on purpose. I usually don't even realize when I am falling into this attitude. It's subtle. It creeps up on me. It affects my feelings toward other churches, toward church members, toward my denominational leaders, toward my own staff, toward my wife, my kids, and myself. I make a mess. God is dealing with me about this right now. Maybe as God deals with my heart today, he will also deal with yours.

I know how you feel. I understand your guilt and shame. I even believe that this moment may change you forever, if you'll stop right here, ask God to reveal his truth, and respond to his call.

Remember one final thing: when you become a mouse, you begin to view everyone else as a cat. When you become a cat, you begin to view everyone else as a mouse. Both are destructive. Don't be either!

Garage-Door Openers

1. Describe some of the mice in the church you lead.

2. List the traits or qualities in your leadership style that release people to approach you with mouse issues. List qualities that prohibit people from approaching you with mouse issues.

3. Are the people in the church you lead walking together in unity? Why or why not?

4. How could you structure your ministry to become more effective?

5. How have you ignored potential mice in the church you lead?

6. Are you more of a mouse or a cat?

Chapter 8

The Back Door:

HEALTHY EXITS FROM THE GARAGE

One of the features commonly included in a garage is a back door. The back door is often required by code for fire-safety purposes. Homeowners use this back door to enter and exit freely without using the bigger garage door.

In church life, we often refer to the back door as the door through which people permanently leave the church. I've been to workshops designed to help pastors "close" the back door of the church they lead. I understand the heart of such workshops and wholeheartedly agree that we need to do all we can to retain people for the growth and health of the church.

> **The problem is, we don't have enough healthy exits through which people can leave.**

However, let's expand our thinking about the back-door concept. Let's start by asking the question, "Is there a time it's healthy for individuals to exit the churches we lead?" Most pastors would say "yes." Some people just don't fit in the churches we lead and never will.

The problem is, we don't have enough healthy exits through which people can leave. Let's consider some of the unhealthy aspects of common church exits.

The people leaving don't tell us they're leaving. Ignorance isn't always bliss. We recently had a garage sale. We set up several large items in the garage and allowed people to browse. One person asked me all about a bed we were selling. He was extremely interested and began making offers. The price we were asking was more than fair, and we explained that we were firm on the price. The buyer said this bed was just what he was looking for, and he would probably take it.

At this point, my wife asked me a question and my attention was needed elsewhere. When I returned to finish the deal with the interested party, he was gone. I saw him driving away in his car. I couldn't believe it. Did I offend him? Did he change his mind? Did he see something about the bed that discouraged him? All of these things went racing through my mind. We ended up selling the bed to the next interested party.

The thing that bothers me to this day is that I have no idea why the man acted so interested in the bed and walked away

> **❝ People in this culture are good at acting interested and asking all the right questions about church. ❞**

without any reason or explanation. Get the point? People in this culture are good at acting interested and asking all the right questions about church. They may come into the garage, listen to your preaching, participate in ministry, sing the music, ask for the details of your programming, and say all the right things. Then they leave. No explanation, no reason, no warning.

I realize people don't owe us an explanation for their exits, especially the unchurched folks that we want to have snooping around the garage. However, it still leaves questions in our minds: Why did they leave? Did we do something wrong?

There's a big difference between a new person coming into the garage, looking around and then deciding to leave, and a person who has been through the garage and entered the house and then decided to leave. People who have been a part of the church for a long time should accept the responsibility to share their reasons for leaving before they exit. However, they may not know that. This is the time for you to become proactive in the process.

When I hear that an involved, committed family or individual has left Timberline Church, I make it a point to give them a call or write them a letter. It's crucial that you or another leader

> **❝ If you don't communicate with people before or after they exit, an open wound will remain without closure. ❞**

in the church communicate with those who exit your church. This communication is not to make people feel guilty for leaving nor to coerce them to return. It's simply so that no wounds remain unclosed. If you don't communicate with people before or after they exit, an open wound will remain without closure.

Unclosed wounds create problems in long-term church credibility and integrity. People who live in smaller communities understand this point best. If you're pastoring in a smaller community, the negative voices of a few families can be damaging, especially over several years.

I've learned that if you take the initiative to contact the person and discover his or her thoughts and reasons for leaving the church (which is never easy), you'll be able to salvage respect and trust the majority of the time. Even when the differences involve major issues and painful experiences, you'll have the opportunity to release them and make some positive statements about the person's future. Let me tell you of one such case.

We received a letter from a family that had been a part of our church for over twenty years. They had given financially, and their kids were grown and involved in church ministries. The letter was short and rigid. It was addressed to our pastors and deacons (at least they knew we stuck together). It made statements that were obviously intended to jar us and hurt us. It gave some examples of issues they had twisted far from the truth. They wanted their names removed from membership. I shared the letter with our pastoral and deacon teams. We prayed for this family and asked God to give us an opportunity to share the correct facts concerning the situation.

I wrote a letter back to them correcting their assumptions and misinformation. It was a firm letter, going straight to the core of the issues. It was kind, but intense. The last paragraph of the letter stated that we had removed them from our membership and were thankful for their many years of faithful involvement. We opened the door to them if they wanted to pursue the facts further. We assured them we would do everything necessary to reveal the truth. The letter was mailed. We've not heard from them since.

Here's the good part of that mess. About three months after that happened, a pastor friend of mine told me a family from Timberline had started attending his church. He stated their name and I braced myself for what he might say next. I was waiting for something like, "They said you were a really lousy pastor and the church was on a road to destruction." But he didn't. He said they had worked through some pain and felt like they needed a different setting that fit their traditions better than Timberline.

He told me they were positive about their new church and had signed up to become prayer partners with him. The issue is settled. If I see them at the mall or the grocery store, I will not

> 66 There are far too many people who have been hurt in church, regardless of fault, but have never had the opportunity to bring the story to an end. Let's be leaders who change this tragic part of ministry. 99

dash into another aisle to avoid a feeling of discomfort. Rather, I will ask them how they are doing with the changes they've made. Am I glad they left? No! Do I realize that they probably needed to leave? Yes!

Unfortunately, not all stories like this have an ending. There are far too many people who have been hurt in church, regardless of fault, but have never had the opportunity to bring the story to an end. Let's be leaders who change this tragic part of ministry.

We've blocked the back door shut. Denver has one of the greatest stock show/rodeo events in the country. Each January, thousands of people from all over the world gather for a variety of events. One of those events always intrigues me. They bring ten to fifteen sheep out into the arena. These sheep are free to move about anywhere they want. They run here and there. Suddenly, out of nowhere, a sheep dog bolts onto the scene. This dog is incredible. It runs from one side of the arena to the other, gathering and chasing these sheep into a little pen that's been set up at one end of the arena. The dog is focused and determined. The dog isn't performing for the crowd; it's doing what it was created to do. Once the dog gets all the sheep back into the pen, it lies down quietly, making certain that not one of those sheep gets out.

I fear that some pastors are like that dog, chasing every sheep that's loose. They run here and there, trying to get all the sheep back in the pen where they belong. All of the energy the pastor has goes into running the sheep back into the garage. Many pastors work so hard to retain everybody, they end up impacting nobody.

> 66 Many pastors work so hard to retain everybody, they end up impacting nobody. 99

You must realize it's actually healthy to allow the back door to swing open as needed. There's a time to help someone open that back door and say goodbye in a healthy way. They'll respect you more for helping them exit in a healthy way than if you chase them all around the yard trying to lock them in the pen.

We've blocked the back door open. Have you ever felt like you had the gift of pushing people out the back door? A friend of mine asked his pastor how he was doing and the pastor answered, "I'm doing great; this church is going down more slowly than any church I've had before."

I remember when I first began to understand how healthy it was to release people who didn't click in our church. I made several statements from the pulpit about some of the great churches in our community and noted that some people should consider going to help them if this church wasn't what they needed. Then I realized how dangerous that was. We must not encourage people toward a consumer mind-set that says, "Go where they do it the way you like it."

> 66 We must not encourage people toward a consumer mind-set that says, 'Go where they do it the way you like it.' 99

I began to understand that some people have come into our garage because they desperately need to be stretched by God. God brought them to us, not so we could release them when they became uncomfortable, but so that we could take them on the stretching journey of faith.

When we launched one of our building campaigns, a gentleman came to me after the service shaking his head. He said that he had just come from a church in another state that had split over a building program. He said he just didn't think he could go through something like that again. I looked at him very confidently and said, "I know why God brought you to this church." His eyes widened, and he asked what I meant by that. I said, "God brought you here so you can be a part of a church that went through a building program without splitting."

> 66 God will often bring people into your garage because they need to be ministered to from your ministry perspective. 99

God will often bring people into your garage because they need to be ministered to from your ministry perspective. This strengthens them as well as the Kingdom of God. Sometimes you need to encourage people to pray again before they decide to leave. Talk openly with them, and be sure no one is missing God's plan. Don't prop open the back door. But let it open when it's needed and maintain a heart for touching people where they are.

Taking Exits Personally

Do you take it personally when someone leaves your church? I sure do. Does it hurt your feelings? It does mine. I hate it. I lose sleep over it. I get mad over it. I vent to my wife over it. My blood pressure is going up as I write this section. Other pastors tell me to get over it. I shake my head and squint my eyes as if to say, "Yeah, I'm gonna forget it." But I never do. I move on; I continue; I grow from it; but I don't really ever forget it. I'm not sure we're supposed to get over it. Maybe we're too good at forgetting it. There must be some kind of a balance here.

> **Care but don't carry.**

God put a phrase in my heart a few years ago that has helped me in this area. The phrase is "Care but don't carry." Jesus Christ was the "carrier" of the burden and we are the "care-ers" of the sheep.

• His hands were nailed down so my hands could reach out.

• His feet were pierced so my feet could be the beautiful feet of good news.

• His body was placed on the cross so my body could take people to it.

• His voice cried out to the Father so my voice could proclaim the gospel.

• His life was taken so mine could be offered.

I encourage you to continue to care about the back door, but don't carry the burdens.

The potential risks that face the church when the pastor gets his or her feelings hurt are serious. The fine line that separates "care" from "carry" is critical. When a pastor personalizes the exit of those whom he has loved, he risks missing the bigger vision God has for his church. Let's look at some common reactions to exits and their risks.

THE "I CAN FIX IT" RESPONSE

The pain of rejection causes us to try to fix the problems quickly without really fixing them at all. We appease to avoid the war. When our feelings get hurt, we often work harder to falsely fix problems or end the conflict because our worth is at stake. Furthermore, when someone goes out of the back door, we don't want anyone else joining him or her.

I've learned that criticism usually has a little bit of truth to it. I don't like this. I don't even like to admit it. I'm tempted at times to make a statement that'll appear to "fix" the problem rather than accept the weakness and work to improve it.

Have you ever been around a "fixer"? They want no conflict, no friction, no tension, and no dialogue that may lead to an argument. They just want to make the whole thing go away.

> **66** People learn quickly whether their pastor avoids conflict. They'll imitate the pastor's personality to protect him. **99**

This passive "Let's get over it without resolving it" attitude is risky because it puts the church in a tension between unity and integrity. People learn quickly whether their pastor avoids conflict. They'll imitate the pastor's personality to protect him. There are many churches in America that have a silent tension that no one will talk about because it might hurt someone's feelings. When the pastor leads from this viewpoint and works quickly to "fix" the problems on the surface without going to their roots, he or she teaches the congregation that this is how to address conflict.

I once sat in a meeting with a church board from another city to help them think through some ways to handle change in their church. When we began talking about a certain subject, the board members began to fidget in their chairs. They looked around at each other with wide eyes and concern. I knew something was up, and I asked them if this was a subject we could discuss. The silence lasted about ten thousand years or so, and finally the designated leader asked the other members of the board, "Should we go ahead and talk about this?" Then another asked, "Should we tell him?"

As the issue unfolded, it became obvious to me and to them that they had not been allowed to vocalize their concerns for a long time. This topic was out-of-bounds for discussion. The issue had caused too much pain in the past and was never really resolved. They were taught, "It's better to drop it than to deal with it."

I realize there's wisdom in choosing proper timing to discuss certain issues with our leadership teams. I want you to consider your style of leadership and ask yourself if there are issues you've tried to "fix" without really dealing with the root of those issues. If you're in this position, pray that God will give you the strength and a healthy plan to bring the situation to a true, genuine close.

Don't keep the leadership teams or the church in a tension between silence and truth. Silence isn't always unity. Refusing to talk about issues will create more tension and deepen the issue. Some teeth need to be filled, others need a root canal. The teeth that need a root canal only need it because they were not filled when the decay was minor.

THE "I'LL SHOW YOU" RESPONSE

The hurt of rejection causes us to become defensive and mean-spirited. We especially become this way if the leaving party says something mean about us on the way out. This is a natural response. It's difficult to hold your tongue or show grace when you've been personally attacked.

> 66 We must not avoid the battles that need to be fought, but we'd better not pick fights that have no purpose. 99

I don't like it when people criticize the church I lead or me. I can easily think of a few things to say about them, so there!

Get it? We quickly get caught up in an unnecessary battle. I said earlier that we must not avoid the battles that need to be fought, but I'll also tell you we'd better not pick fights that have no purpose.

One of my good friends in junior high used to say, "No matter how tough you are, there's always someone who can beat you up." I think maybe God allowed me to hear that enough as a kid so I would be able to remember it when I became a pastor. About the time I feel confident and strong, it seems someone bigger wants to pick a fight. I assure you, I can still be beaten up pretty badly.

When pastors fall into the "I'll show you" trap, we accept the challenge of the fight. We put up our fists and prepare for the battle. We use our place of position and authority to beat the devil out of people. The problem is, it may be the devil in us that needs to be beaten out.

We often take this mean, attacking spirit to the pulpit with us. We're short with our families, and we complain to others. We plant seeds of logic to justify our dislike of these people and teach our followers how to Christianize a grudge. We hold on to the pain and look for every opportunity to tell people "the real story" about why those people left.

If I had been Jesus, I would have used my power to quiet the crowds. Can you imagine being Christ and having all the power of deity at your disposal? Can you imagine standing before some insignificant king who is trying to determine your fate? Not me, buddy; I would have thrown around a few lightning bolts and brought on a few claps of thunder. Some soldier spitting in my face and pulling out my hair would have brought a couple of meteorites crashing down on his head.

Let's face it, you and I probably have the power to crush a few backdoor escapees. We have the board meeting. We have the pastoral team (who are paid to be loyal). We have the pulpit. Now that's power. Will we "show 'em?" Or will we "show them the way"? Proverbs 15:1a says, "A gentle answer turns away wrath." Wow! Check your heart. Check your spirit. Check your mind. Then you'll be ready to check back into the game.

> 66 Will we 'show 'em?' Or will we 'show them the way'? 99

THE "I DON'T CARE" RESPONSE

Apathy is a powerful and noticeable attitude. It's not silent; apathy screams loudly and leaves an echo in the room after you leave the building. The "I don't care" attitude is developed in our lives slowly. It has many places of birth. Let's look at them:

> 66 It's not that you don't care; you simply act as if you don't care because you can't take any more hurt from the issue. 99

Birthing Room 1: Pain

Enough pain caused by people exiting through the back door creates the "I don't care" attitude. It's not that you don't care; you simply act as if you don't care because you can't take any more hurt from the issue.

Different personalities respond differently to pain. I have a friend in our city who pastors a great church. They were going through some changes in their ministry philosophy. Some of these changes weren't embraced by some of the established people of the church. They began to exit—family after family.

I called the pastor to see how he was doing. I was so proud of him when he said, "It's really painful; we'll miss these great people, but we're moving in the right direction." I hung up the phone and realized that he would make it through this time as long as he kept that attitude.

> 66 Being able to feel pain is actually a gift of leadership. 99

Being able to feel pain is actually a gift of leadership. I recently went to the dentist (not something I do that often). I'm in the process of getting two caps put on my teeth. I've never been through this experience before and have come to understand why I avoid the dentist. My last visit was interesting because they had to keep injecting the substance that numbs your mouth, tooth, jaw, and face. I had about three times the normal dose of this stuff.

About the time the dentist finished up, I was numb. I mean really numb. He warned me to be careful not to eat anything for a few hours until the feeling returned. He said there was a strong chance I would chew the inside of my cheek and not even know it. I would not even feel my teeth biting down on my tongue or my cheek. Incredible! I was careful and needed no plastic surgery to repair my face.

The point is this: Sometimes when we get so numb to the pain of people exiting the church, we chew through things that should not be chewed on at all. We do damage that cannot be easily repaired.

Pain is birthed in our lives when we face issues we can't resolve. Pain cuts our hearts, creating scabs. The tissue becomes tougher than before it was ripped. The second time our hearts are torn, the tissue grows back even tougher again, and again, and again. Finally the resistance to the hurt in our lives has grown to such a level that we really don't care. We no longer feel the pain. My prayer is that we will always feel the pain!

We need to find a way to keep the same pain from recurring. The constant recurrence of the hurt over people who exit the church can be dealt with practically and effectively. I want to recommend two things:

• **Come to an understanding of the type of people you're most likely to reach.** Every church has a personality. This is not an evil thing. The body of Christ is large and diverse. We need to embrace our diversity rather than despise it.

When certain people have exited our church, it's been helpful to step back and realize how different their philosophy of ministry is from mine. Sometimes I've shaken my head and said, "I can't believe they stayed in our church as long as they did." They're to be commended. When I understand this, it takes away the effect of the repeating jab in my face.

> **"** Sometimes I've shaken my head and said, 'I can't believe they stayed in our church as long as they did.' They're to be commended. **"**

My perspective is different now. I want people to be fulfilled, not frustrated. Some people who are troublemakers in one church can be an incredible blessing in another. They fit in better. Release them and view it as a benefit to the Kingdom of God, not another slap in your face.

• **Accept that some people lack wholehearted commitment.** Our culture is dying from the inside out. People will not make a long-term commitment like they used to. This is impacting every aspect of life—employment, marriage, parenting, and so on.

I'm amazed at how big the front door of our church gets when we do productions and outreaches and then how big the back door gets when we enter a building campaign or push for a commitment. I've had to release people to exit who I really thought were locked into the vision. When I realize the lack of commitment in our culture, it eases the pain. It isn't always something I've done.

> **"** I'm amazed at how big the front door of our church gets when we do productions and outreaches and then how big the back door gets when we enter a building campaign or push for a commitment. **"**

Birthing Room 2: Pride

I've watched on a few occasions what happens when a church grows to a significant level and the pastor or leadership team begins to take exits for granted.

The "I don't care" attitude grips them because they really don't think they need the people who are leaving. This attitude says, "Don't let the door hit you on your way out." It's an attitude of arrogance and pride.

God will not continue to bless a church or a pastor that maintains a prideful attitude. I believe we need to take the Bible seriously when it says to "Humble yourselves before the Lord" (James 4:10a). I think what that really means is, "Humble yourself before God humbles you."

If every church in my community of about 150,000 people was filled to capacity on Sunday morning, there would still be about 130,000 people at home. I don't think any church in America can boast of reaching its entire city yet.

The point is, we need to keep seeing the need around us. A faithful pastor will notice the people who are not coming more than the people who are. This keeps us on our knees and living in reality.

Birthing Room 3: Weariness

This is probably the greatest cause of falling into the "I don't care" trap. When you're tired, you don't care. Bonnie and I have laughed through the years at how differently we respond to our kids when we are very tired. "OK, drink the pop; we don't want to argue about it at midnight." "Sure, do whatever—just don't wake us up."

There are times in my life when I become so weary that someone going out of the back door just doesn't matter to me. I have no energy left to go after him or her.

When Jesus told the story of the lost sheep in Luke 15:4-6, he said some haunting things:

"Suppose one of you has a hundred sheep and loses one of them. Does he not leave the ninety-nine in the open country and go after the lost sheep until he finds it? And when he finds it, he joyfully puts it on his shoulders and goes home. Then he calls his friends and neighbors together and says, 'Rejoice with me; I have found my lost sheep.' "

When we're weary, we usually think of a few thoughts like, "I'm glad it's only one sheep. So long." Or "I can think of a few others I wish would leave." Jesus even said that once the shepherd found the lost sheep, "he joyfully puts it on his shoulders." Whoa! I think when I'm weary I would give that sheep a piece of my mind. I would drag it back to the pen and make it an example for the rest of the sheep.

Have you ever been there? Maybe you're there now. I've only found one remedy in my life for weariness. It's fairly simple. It's not too risky if you want to try it. When I become weary, burdened, and tired of being a shepherd, I become a sheep, and the Good Shepherd always comes to find me.

> **When I become weary, burdened, and tired of being a shepherd, I become a sheep, and the Good Shepherd always comes to find me.**

Choosing Doors

To finalize our thoughts concerning the back door, I want you to think about one other thing. The typical garage has a back door, but it also has another door. I'm not talking about the big garage door; I'm talking about the door in the garage that leads into the house.

We'll talk about this other door in the next chapter. But I want you to understand that when people have hung out in the garage for a while, they eventually have to make a decision. It's not always an easy decision. It may take a few months or for some, even a few years. But eventually they'll decide whether to go into the house.

If people decide not to go into the house and become real family members, they'll eventually go to the back door and exit the garage. You must be satisfied that you were a part of helping individuals come to a decision about which house they'll enter and live in. It's possible they'll enter a different church and find their way into the house. We can only pray that God will continue to lead and guide them. Ultimately, it's their decision.

> **You must be satisfied that you were a part of helping individuals come to a decision about which house they'll enter and live in.**

159

Garage-Door Openers

1. How could you better utilize the back door in the church you lead?

2. Do you try to keep the back door shut and locked? Why or why not?

3. Do you tend to keep the back door wide open and swinging? Why or why not?

4. Do people exiting your church typically tell you first? Why or why not?

5. What are some ways you can help people achieve closure when they exit your church?

6. Do you typically "care" or "carry"? How has this affected your ministry?

7. Are you weary in your ministry right now? What changes can you make in order to gain back your vigor?

Chapter 9

The Other Door:
INVITING PEOPLE INSIDE THE HOUSE

We've taken a look at the back door in the garage. Now let's take a good look at the "other door" in the garage. If you have a garage that's attached to your house, then you have one of these doors. It's the door that leads into the house.

The garage is safe because there are so many exits, and the big door is easy to find. Unchurched people like that and need that. I've watched literally hundreds of people go into the garage of our church. I've watched them wander around, examine the tools, feel the benches, and look at the detail.

I've been amazed as each unchurched person watches God's family go in and out of the other door. They're curious about this door. It's a door that scares them. It's a door they know will call to them one day. It'll open and they'll be invited to enter in. As these souls stand in the garage, they explore what it means to go into the house.

Many unchurched people have never really been in this kind of house—a house where love is lived out and truth is modeled. They watch as others go through the other door with their messy lives, their sin, their shame, and their sorrow. They've witnessed with their own eyes as these same people have been transformed, renewed, and charged by God with a new mission for life. It's alarming to them. It's mysterious. How can these people go through that door so needy and hungry and come out so filled and empowered?

Over time, seekers catch a glimpse of the truth. They've stood by the other door long enough to look inside and catch a momentary glimpse of the person responsible for building the house. They've heard about this person, but they've never really met or fully believed in him. They're curious about what others have claimed about him: "He's changed my life! I'm free. I'm forgiven." They've examined and questioned this person's claims and have come to the same conclusions seekers of Jesus did while he walked the earth, conclusions such as:

- "I find no fault in him."
- "Surely, this man was the Son of God."
- "Sir, give me this water so that I won't get thirsty."

> 66 I've seen people stand by the other door just so they could feel their heart be tugged toward the truth on the other side. They want to believe. 99

Seekers are intrigued by Jesus' claims and his life, and the other door keeps drawing them closer and closer.

I've seen people stand by the other door just so they could feel their heart be tugged toward the truth on the other side. They want to believe; they hope it's true; they long for a voice to call their names and invite them to enter the house.

Finally, it happens. It's almost as though they've been standing with an ear pressed tightly against the door, trying to hear the voice. The door opens wide and they're finally exposed to God himself. The maker of the house whispers their names. He invites them to come in. This is the biggest moment of their lives. It's often a moment of complete and utter brokenness and is often blurred by tears. Other times it's a moment of such enlightenment and fulfillment that there are no words at all.

But it's always a moment of truth.

It's always a moment of faith.

It's always a moment of change.

The other door in the garage leads into the house. Let's try to understand the significance of the house.

The House Is a Place of Safety

Why do Christians come together and worship God? Why do they leave the comfort of their homes and drive to a place where they'll face the parking lot, the cold, the heat, the standing, the sitting, the preaching, the music, and the challenges? Why do people go in the other door and spend time, money, and energy for such a cause?

> 66 God created needs in people that push them toward the other door and into the house. 99

The spiritual need is a strong, driving force in the human soul. God created needs in people that push them toward the other door and into the house. People long for a safe environment in which to grow, stretch, and participate.

Safety has become a commodity in this culture. We've seen violence impact our schools, homes, neighborhoods, and cities, causing people to withdraw and isolate themselves. People need to have a place of spiritual safety.

I can recall moments in my childhood when I was awakened in the night by noises that were unfamiliar. I would lie and listen. I could feel my heart beating within my chest. The silence would become as bad as the noise.

My mind would imagine all kinds of creatures walking through my doorway. The shadows on the wall seemed to become some evil thing that wanted to take my life. My bedroom was just across the hall from my parents' room. I knew if I could just make it into their room, the monster would leave me alone and I would be safe. The journey to get there would be the struggle. I would muster all my courage and bolt across the hall into my parents' room and into their bed. That was the greatest moment of all. It was almost worth being afraid just to have that moment of climbing into that warm, safe bed.

> 66 The house of God should always be a spiritually safe place. 99

Think of all the people in the garage who are afraid. They really want to come through a door that will lead them to safety. The house of God should always be a spiritually safe place. Here are some ways the church should be safe:

• **It should be safe to ask dumb questions.** Some people are brilliant in their field of expertise but completely ignorant about God. I'm stunned at the people who find Christ but have never owned or read a Bible. The stories of Moses, Elijah, and David seem completely foreign to them. They need an environment where it's safe to ask the questions that seem silly or elementary to us. Let's make certain we know how to keep our teaching and preaching simple when we have new people coming into the house.

• **It should be safe to confess sin.** The need to confess sin has never been greater than right now. If we're not careful, we'll forget the value of people confessing their faults to one another. New believers need to feel safe to share their hearts and their pasts with another. This environment should be part of the house. God is the one who needs to hear our confessions. But people overcome sin issues more quickly when it's safe to share them with others.

• **It should be safe to bring a friend.** I always liked bringing friends over to my house. My mom was the cool mom of the neighborhood who knew how to love everybody. Our house was like the neighborhood fort. We had boundaries, but we also had real freedom.

> **❝ How many churches have cultivated an environment that's safe enough to invite a friend into? ❞**

I was saddened when one of my neighborhood buddies brought me into his house but had to sneak me in because his mother was an alcoholic. She wouldn't let guests in the house after school. This was her time to drink. I had a difficult time trying to understand this problem. It was foreign to me. I had no way of identifying with it.

How many churches have cultivated an environment that's safe enough to invite a friend into? The house should be a place that opens its arms to those who have never been inside before.

• **It should be safe enough to live.** This may sound kind of strange at first, but I think it'll make sense as we discuss it. I'm not talking about physical life and death. I'm talking about the freedom to develop your spiritual personality.

Bonnie and I have three children, and we're amazed at how different they are from each other. It doesn't seem possible that they could be from the same family and yet be so unique and different.

It's fulfilling to observe your children having enough sense of safety to experiment with their own personality development. When kids feel safe in their home environment, they'll express many of life's emotions. The freedom to live is their openness to laugh, cry, or be silly. It releases the spontaneous. It allows for the unrehearsed and it enjoys the moment. The same should be true in the church.

The House Is a Place of Connection

I have four sisters, and we're all very close. I love them dearly and have been blessed by God through them. One of the great benefits of coming through the other door is that you'll find so many wonderful spiritual brothers and sisters to connect with.

I cannot think of a greater place to connect with people than church. When you look at our world, you'll notice that it loves to party. Think of all the money, time, and energy that go into events like the Super Bowl and New Year's Eve celebrations. People love events like these because they're an excuse to be connected and to feel connected.

People inside the house should understand the power of greeting and connecting with people who are coming through the other door. When a church walks in connectedness, it will impact people's lives.

Think about the church you lead. Does it have some good parties? Do the people in the house believe they're connected to each other? I'm not talking about knowing everybody or being best friends with everyone. I'm talking about having a sense of family and closeness. I'm talking about that joy of knowing we're having Family Night and looking forward to it. Do people smile when they show up because they anticipate a great experience with God and his children?

> **The church should know how to party.**

The church should know how to party. I don't mean in a worldly sense. I'm talking about the joy of family laughter, family celebration, family birthday parties, family rewards, and family connection.

Many of the people who finally walk through the other door will be walking into the first true family experience they've ever had. Let's make sure it's a good one.

> **Don't be discouraged if certain people don't like certain ministries. Ministries are simply rooms, each with a different purpose.**

The House Is a Place of Many Rooms

I'll try not to go off the deep end with this room concept, but consider for a moment all of the different rooms in a house. Each room has a different function. When people come through the other door, they'll find many rooms to look into. This is a great way for them to see the diversity and variety in the house.

They'll like some rooms more than others. This is a good thing. Don't be discouraged if certain people don't like certain ministries. Ministries are simply rooms, each with a different purpose.

One of the disappointments for many new Christians who walk through the other door is the lack of creativity we've offered in the ministries of the church. In most churches, if you don't sing or play an instrument, the only job left for you is teaching a class—the preschool class. No thank you! The different rooms in the house need to be specific and unique. They need to be decorated in ways that allow new people the opportunity to find one that appeals to them.

Ministry ideas are everywhere. What would happen if we asked everyone in our church over the weekend to write down one idea for a ministry they've thought about but haven't developed? I wonder how many great ideas we would have. Let me share a few unique ideas for ministry that people in our church have thought of:

> 66 The moment new Christians walk through the other door, they have a wonderful meal provided for them. They sit down at the table and begin to take in nourishment for their souls. This nourishment is the truth of God's Word and the power of the Holy Spirit working in their lives. 99

• Teaching senior adults how to use a computer and the Internet

• Teaching Internet-based discipleship classes in a chat room

• Creating Christian-based clubs for reaching bikers, cyclists, race-car drivers, moms, dads, skaters, homeless people, ex-prisoners, affluent people, executives, media personnel, and so on

• Providing transportation for people who need it

• Hosting art shows with Christian themes

• Doing maintenance on the church facility

• Helping with new construction for additions and deletions on the church facility

Get people to put some energy into thinking about the different possible rooms in your house. It may be time to remodel your ministry.

The House Is a Place of Nourishment

The other door in the garage often goes directly or almost directly into the kitchen/eating area. This is a wonderful parallel. The moment new Christians walk through the other door, they have a splendid meal provided for them. They sit down at the table and begin to take in nourishment for their souls. This nourishment is the truth of God's Word and the power of the Holy Spirit working in their lives.

I love the story of Peter and the other disciples fishing on the lake in John 21:4-6. I like it because they weren't catching any fish, just like me when I go fishing.

"Early in the morning, Jesus stood on the shore, but the disciples did not realize that it was Jesus. He called out to them, 'Friends, haven't you any fish?' 'No,' they answered. He said, 'Throw your net on the right side of the boat and you will find some.' When they did, they were unable to haul the net in because of the large number of fish."

When they reached the shore, Jesus had a nice little fire burning and cooked up a tasty breakfast. He fed the disciples spiritually and physically.

People in our churches need to be nourished and strengthened every time they walk through the door. Here's a snapshot of how a shepherd nourishes a flock, drawn from Psalm 23:1-6.

• **"The Lord is my shepherd, I shall not be in want."** The shepherd's presence brings contentment and fulfillment because of a long-term relationship built on trust.

• **"He makes me lie down in green pastures."** The shepherd gives forethought and planning to the destination of the sheep. The shepherd knows the value of green pastures and of lying down.

• **"He leads me beside quiet waters."** The shepherd knows the difference between troubled waters and quiet waters. The shepherd leads; the shepherd doesn't push; the shepherd's words are bathed in kindness; and the shepherd values peace.

- **"He restores my soul."** The shepherd restores those who have been plundered, abused, or wounded. The shepherd restores them because the shepherd doesn't remain in the past, but draws the sheep toward a new and adventurous future.
- **"He guides me in paths of righteousness for his name's sake."** The shepherd has high ethical standards for living. The shepherd knows the path and gently walks there, willing to be a guide rather than a dictator.
- **"Even though I walk through the valley of the shadow of death, I will fear no evil, for you are with me."** The shepherd understands the dark valleys and the shadows of doubt, fear, and discouragement. The shepherd isn't afraid, and the sheep don't get spooked. The shepherd doesn't deny the reality of danger but remains steadfast on the path.
- **"Your rod and your staff, they comfort me."** The shepherd does not use authority in an abusive manner. The shepherd finds the tools necessary to cultivate healthy, vibrant relationships. The sheep don't fear the shepherd's presence. They love it when the shepherd walks throughout the flock.
- **"You prepare a table before me in the presence of my enemies."** The shepherd protects the flock from the predators lurking over them and feeds them nourishing food. The shepherd knows how to calm the sheep even in nervous and tense situations. The shepherd doesn't live in denial but lives confidently in reality.
- **"You anoint my head with oil; my cup overflows."** The shepherd sees to it that the sheep have the oil poured out upon them. This keeps them clean, pure, and healthy. The abundance of care creates enough strength to release the flock from the panic of loneliness.
- **"Surely goodness and love will follow me all the days of my life, and I will dwell in the house of the Lord forever."** The shepherd teaches sheep to look forward. The shepherd helps them feel secure enough to press on without fear.

This is our calling. This is our mantle, and nothing less is required as we tend and nourish Christ's church.

The House Is a Place of Education

Many families in America have taken on the challenge of home-schooling their children. While Bonnie and I have not attempted this from a scholastic viewpoint, we do believe that we're responsible for the process of education in our home.

Christians desperately need to be educated. We have a great opportunity to educate people when they walk through the other door into the house. Start with a simple list I call the "BASICS."

B—Bible The Bible is truly our road map. We must teach people the Word of God.

A—Attributes of God People need to discover who God is and what he is like.

S—Spirit of God Help people understand the convicting, transforming, and comforting role of the Holy Spirit.

I—Identify in Christ...Who I am! People need to find out who they really are in Christ—forgiven, clean, empowered, and released.

C—Calling...What I do! Ministry that is done from a sense of calling from God will be fulfilling and contagious.

S—Sin...What it is and how to overcome it! Once people understand what sin really is, they can grasp the truth about forgiveness.

The House Is a Place of Love

I'm always saddened to learn about the people who grew up in homes that didn't model or exemplify true love. What a tragedy! This has created a real challenge for the church. Many people entering our doors have never been around a healthy, functional family. This means they're going to be shocked and alarmed at the care we show for one another. They don't understand family commitment or family loyalty. These may be the very things these people need, but they are often slow to respond as family participants.

I challenge you to love again. Love God. Love Deacons and Elders. Love your flock. Walk through the hallways instead of going to your study. Hang around, be available. If you model this, others will follow. When people begin to sense love from God and from the Church, they will respond to others in a loving manner. It's that simple.

Finally, remind your church how important it is to love one another. Talk about the loving little things like holding the doors for people behind you, giving your bulletin to a stranger, letting another car exit ahead of you from the parking lot, and smiling and saying hi to strangers. When the house becomes a place of love, the other stuff we've been talking about in this book works!

Conclusion

People in this generation and in the years that lie ahead are less likely to enter a church than at any time in our history. America needs revival. The simple concept of "opening the garage door" hopefully will bring unchurched people into this incredible house of God. I believe that we are called by God to do what we can do to reach lost people in our culture for the Kingdom of God.

May this great God who called you
...keep you broken enough to mend others.
...keep you well enough to enjoy others.
...keep you hungry enough to feed others.
...keep you wondering enough to find the lost.
...keep you secure enough to present the truth.
...keep you home enough to enjoy the blessings.
...keep you out enough to see the broken.
...keep you fresh enough to inspire others.
...keep you weary enough to remain anchored in him.
...keep you blind enough to believe him anyway.
...keep you real enough to be touched by the hurting.
...keep you numb enough to endure the storm.
...keep you sensitive enough to feel others' pain.
...keep you weeping enough to remain dependent.

...keep you joyful enough to continue on.
...keep you strong enough to reach the weak.
...keep you weak enough to reach out to the strong.
And most of all, may my God
...keep you growing and changing.

Garage-Door Openers

1. What cultivates a hunger in unchurched people to go through the other door in your church?

2. Identify some people you've watched come through that door. Describe the process.

3. Identify some people who are looking at the door but have not entered. What do you feel is holding them back?

4. What are some ways you can become more intentional and strategic in getting people through the other door in your church?

5. Describe the house that you are inviting people into currently. What can you do to make your house warmer and more inviting to newcomers?